"A game-changer for flipping the script on failing, setbacks, and even doubts about the future. If you want to upgrade your work and your life, read this book."
—Keith Ferrazzi, *New York Times* Bestselling Author, *Never Eat Alone*

"Failing (and learning from it) has been the key to my success in Ninja Warrior and everything I've ever excelled at. I read Alex's book at the perfect time to remind me that it applies to all areas of my life—especially the scary new goals that don't come easily. And Alex can show you how to do it!"
—Jessie Graff, Top American Ninja Warrior, Professional Stuntwoman

"I've always connected with Alex's passion, positive energy, and how he changes people's lives. You need to get past failures to reach high goals, and Alex will take you to the next level!"
—Julian Holguin, President of *Billboard*

"This book is perfect for Leaders, Organizations, and Individuals looking to elevate their achievements, gain a competitive edge, and build a culture of perseverance. All coming from an expert speaker, entertainer, and American Ninja Warrior!"
—Josh Linkner, *New York Times* Bestselling Author, 5x Tech Entrepreneur

"Alex is the real deal. The tools he provides to become *Fail Proof* are invaluable for anyone in any area of their life. A great addition to my library, and reminder of the value of persistence and believing in yourself. A must read."

—Kent Weed, Creator & Executive Producer, NBC *American Ninja Warrior*

"Confidence is a non-negotiable for success. Alex gives you a system to create real confidence and grow your self-belief in what is possible for you. Highly recommend!"

—Heather Monahan, Confidence Expert & Bestselling Author

"For me, failing has been so valuable because it has taught me so much about myself. I've seen Alex's growth with Ninja Warrior since the beginning. I've seen his fails, but then I saw him become a real competitor in this sport, and he's got a system to get better—and get results."

—Joe Moravsky, Top American Ninja Warrior

"If you want to level up your leadership and performance to get amazing results, then get this book. Alex delivers real, actionable steps to make goals happen in record time. All with honest and hilarious stories of Alex putting his money where his mouth is! Pick up this book, and crush your goals."

—Anthony Trucks, NFL Pro, Speaker, and Performance Coach

FAIL PROOF

BECOME THE *UNSTOPPABLE* YOU

ALEX WEBER

INTERNATIONAL SPEAKER ∎ AWARD-WINNING ENTERTAINER ∎ AMERICAN NINJA WARRIOR

Foreword by **DR. HENRY CLOUD** *New York Times* Bestselling Author

Post Hill
PRESS

Contents

FAIL PROOF RESILIENCE: BEING UNSTOPPABLE

LOVE YOUR MOMENTS, LOVE YOUR LIFE

This book is dedicated to *you*.

Foreword

By Dr. Henry Cloud
New York Times Bestselling Author

I could almost sum up this foreword to Alex's book by quoting him directly. In one sentence, he nearly said it all:

"To this day, diving in the deep end—regardless of results, judgments, or even looking silly—is the biggest express route to reaching your goals."

This is a key statement, and sums up a lot about what "getting better" is all about: just doing it. To get better, we must "do it." But...as the rest of the book explains so well, "just doing it" is harder than it sounds, and is so hard, in fact, that many people don't dive in. Or they do, and the ugly beast called "failure" steps in and squashes their future before it is ever able to fully take root and grow into greatness.

Alex has given a great guide to keep that "squashing" from happening. He provides the tools to take "failure" and turn it into what it actually is, from my perspective: learning. But, in order to learn, we must see incremental steps of getting better as what learning is all about. The reason that most people cannot learn how to get better has nothing to do with their level of talent or technical expertise in their field of performance, but has everything to do with what is inside their heads—and hearts. It is the internal software that enables them to dive in, and then to keep swimming. And those people find that "the one who swims, usually makes it."

Sometimes I read performance or leadership books that are rooted in someone's personal experience and a "let me share what worked for me" perspective by the author. And usually, I get something out of those books because there must be some truth in their story...after all, "it worked" for him or her. But most of the time, as a professional performance coach, I would rather read books that come from the research and science domain and give more objective, research-based, and scientifically grounded principles than just one person's journey. Usually, the science books contain information and principles that have been proven and scaled to be helpful to more than just one person's experience. Both are useful, but I love empirical research.

Not that people's stories aren't valuable and important, but they can be a bit subjective. Often the author can believe that what worked for them was caused by "a" when a real scientist would tell you that the reason it worked was actually "b." The author got a great result but is now teaching an incomplete or misguided principle that is not going to work for everyone else. Armchair psychology does have its limitations.

What I liked so much about Alex's book is that it does both very well: it shares a subjective story we can learn from, but it also agrees with so much proven science. It is certainly rooted in his own story as both an overcomer and a high achiever—the path he espouses "worked for him." And as I said above, I love hearing people's stories of success and what they learned as they "got there." I always gain something from those personal stories...or at least am inspired to do better myself. But also, as I read his personal story, I was struck, as a psychologist, by how much of what he was sharing agrees with so much of the science of how people perform—or how they don't. He shows in simple language how failure succumbs to the power of emotional dysregulation—the power of the internal voices, the diminishing of motivation, or the tendency to feel "all is lost." Throughout this book, he gets the science right. His book and path not only worked for him, but the research says that the principles he shares can work for you too. They have been proven beyond just his personal story.

So much of performance is mental. There is no shortage of talent or brains in the world, but there are far less accomplished people in the world than there are talented people. Accomplishment requires talent, technical expertise...AND that "immaterial" internal software package that becomes the operating system to make it all work. By "immaterial," do I mean "heart?" "Mind?" "Soul?" Yep....it is all three. And Alex has given us a guide, so you can upgrade your software to get past what today feels like "failure" and move into who and what YOU were created to be. Thanks, Alex!

Dr. Henry Cloud
Los Angeles, 2021

Author's Note

This book is for you if you want *more*.

This book is for you if you've ever faced failure, or if you've ever been knocked down, defeated, or held back by your fears. If you've ever felt unsure of yourself, dealt with a lack of confidence, or struggled with self-belief, then this book is for you too. If you've had doubts, been frustrated, criticized, or gone after something or someone and fallen short. If you ever feel like you're trudging through a swamp of negativity and judgments are being hurled at your head, all while meaner and louder judgments are coming from inside your head...well, then this book is for you, too.

More than anything, this book is for you if you don't want to give up on yourself because you know there is more out there for you. You want more for your work, you want more for your relationships, and you want more for your life. Good! We will make that happen for you. I've given my life to figuring out, guinea pigging, proving, and delivering this system to you right now, because I want to make you unstoppable. I want to give you what I needed in my pivotal moments, what I wish I had.

There is a way to unlock the Unstoppable You, and this is it. I created the Fail Proof System so no matter what comes your way, you won't quit on yourself or give up on your highest goals. Instead, you'll fuel yourself with positive energy; take big, bold actions; and fully commit (and recommit) to yourself.

You'll grow, improve, bounce back, and emerge stronger, better, and smarter than you ever thought possible.

> **You'll surprise yourself with what you can do, who you can become, and how you can lead.**

And you'll make a profound impact on those around you, because when you're unstoppable, other people take notice.

Together, through this book, we will help you do things you didn't believe you could do, become someone you weren't sure you could be, and lead people you never thought you could lead.

We will make you unstoppable.

We will make you Fail Proof.

WELCOME TO YOUR FAIL PROOF LIFE

Welcome To Your Fail Proof Life

_____

"The biggest commitment you must keep
is your commitment to yourself."
—Neale Donald Walsch, Bestselling Author

What would you do if you couldn't fail? What could you do? Who would you become? How might you lead?

You don't need to answer those questions right now; just allow yourself to expand with possibilities. Let those beautiful, wild stallions of ideas run free. We'll be harnessing them shortly.

Let's answer this question first: Why do we hate failing so much? On the surface, it's obvious. Failing is discouraging, frustrating, and embarrassing. It feels horrible to perform poorly, and it also makes us feel horribly about ourselves. If we dig a little deeper, it really makes us feel inadequate, like there's something wrong with us. "Why can't

> **Why do we hate failing so much?**

I do this? I want to be doing it, and I'm not. What's wrong with me? Am I the worst person ever?" Failing erodes our self-belief, destroys our confidence, and gives us this deep fear that we're not capable of doing what needs to be done—and worse, we may not be able to do it in the future for ourselves and for the people who need us to succeed. That's scary. This feeling is only heightened when we see other people succeeding. "How are they doing it? And what do they think of me now that they know I can't do it?" It feels like we're going to be exiled from the society of successful people, branded a failure, and sent off to Failure Island where we'll probably fail there, too. The whirlwind of these feelings is all very real, which is probably why people look at me funny when I tell them I'm an expert at failing.

I've even been called an **expert failer**, and I take it as a huge compliment! To me, it means a willingness to embrace challenges, be bold, fearless, bravely honest, relentless, strong, resilient, ambitious, and confident. It may seem counterintuitive that failing spurs such positive words, but anyone who has accomplished anything meaningful, impressive, and long-lasting knows how to harness failing as a powerful, and uplifting force to success.

You could say I've made a career out of failing, and I'd agree. But really, I've made myself Fail Proof. The Fail Proof System, the one I'm going to share with you in this book, unlocked my career, my relationships, and my life. It has allowed me to become an international keynote speaker, positively impacting over 3.5 million people worldwide. It has powered me to compete on NBC's Emmy-nominated *American Ninja Warrior*, dubbed one of the most difficult physical competitions on Earth. I can attest to that! I used it as a coach, winning championships and becoming one of the youngest to ever achieve US Lacrosse Coach of the Year honors in my very first season. I even relied on it to achieve a breakthrough World Record and become an award-winning host for NBC. It's also allowed me to have more meaningful connections with the people in my life and even a deeper sense of self-worth. Every chapter of my life has driven me to this point, and I'm so excited to give you the best of it right here, right now. I'll be opening up to you about my uplifting wins, my humbling losses, and the *interesting* (and very entertaining) moments in between. I'll also share incredible examples of "fails" from successful people across different industries and walks of life, and I'll even give you the same game-changing lessons, tools, and techniques I present to audiences around the world.

Failing is what stands in the way of our success, and it's among the worst feelings we can ever experience. Failure is even one of the greatest fears on earth.[1] You hear that, spiders?

> **Whether it's falling short of your dreams, losing a must-have deal at work, or getting rejected by someone we love, failing *hurts*.**

It hurts deep down in our guts—that uneasy, queasy feeling where our confidence plummets, we question everything about ourselves, and second-guess all of our goals. Our ruthless inner voice starts turning up the volume on some pretty hurtful things too. "You can't do this. Why did you even try? Stop now, it's never going to happen!" I left out all the merciless name-calling too. The failure makes us want to back away from our obstacles, give in to our fears, and quit on our goals—or worse, quit on ourselves. No wonder we go out of our way to avoid failing, even if that means never trying in the first place.

I get it. I know the feeling well. I know what it feels like to question yourself and lose your self-belief. It feels like your lifeblood has been sucked out of you, and you're a half-inflated shell of who you know you can be. And that feeling doesn't exist in a vacuum; it infiltrates every area of your life. It hurts at work, in relationships, and even when you're alone—sometimes especially when you're alone.

And that's why I'm here. Failing used to be my greatest fear, too. It would cripple me so much I'd be scared to take any action at all for fear of falling short or getting judged. The fear of failing became so great that I would stop taking leaps at all, and as many people do, I began to resign myself to what was comfortable and safe. But before long, it felt like I was lowering the brightness on myself in all areas of my life. I was nervous and hesitant to take action in my work, I felt less confident around my colleagues and my friends, and I even became less connected to the person that I loved. My performance suffered across my life, which only then validated my fears of failing even more, and it wasn't long until I stopped caring for myself all together. It was this awful, slippery slope sliding me off a cliff, and it all began because I was scared to trust in myself and commit to what I wanted.

The torture was that I could see the other me. I could see myself full of confidence and excitement and self-belief doing all the things I wanted to do! I knew it could be real, but *still*, I was too scared to make it happen. And so those moments that could have been…simply never were. Failing and the fear of failing robbed me of moments of my life that I can never get back, and that's why I'm so fired up to share this with you now. I don't want you to miss out on anything you want to do, the person you want to become, and the leader you're capable of being. Failure no longer stands in the way of who I want to be, what I want to do, and the life I want to lead. I have become Fail Proof, and I promise you will become Fail Proof, too.

> **We're going to take that dimmer off your brightness, get your lifeblood pumping, and bring the Unstoppable You to this world!**

BORN OUT OF SOGGY MOMENTS

The Fail Proof System was born out of my toughest moments. I uncovered this system because I needed it—badly! It was in the moments of feeling defeated, beaten down, overwhelmed, underperforming, and scared about my future that I needed it the most. In fact, my dream job was hanging in the balance, and I was afraid that I was going to lose my career, my community, and my sense of self. I gave absolutely everything I had to figuring out this system, and in turn, the system gave me everything back. It gave me confidence, clarity, and a deep commitment to myself, my dream goals, and the people in my life. This Fail Proof System transformed my life, and that's what it will do for you too.

Here's the origin story.

I competed on NBC's *American Ninja Warrior* for the first time in 2019. Have you seen that show before? It's an amazing competition series, Emmy-nominated, and as I write this to you is in its thirteenth season. It's also inspired a rapidly growing sport around the world. The sport has exploded so much, in fact, that hundreds of thousands of people apply to compete each season, and only a few hundred are given the opportunity. When you do get the incredible and rare chance to compete, you take on obstacles which are hidden from you, until the moment you hit them—or they hit you. You don't know the new challenges that will decide your fate until you step on the course to take them on. No other sport is like that! To succeed, you tackle these absurdly difficult, aerial obstacles where you cling by your fingertips to dangling, spinning, and oddly-shaped grips, ropes, and rings—and then you fling yourself through the air to cling by your fingertips onto yet more dangling, spinning, and oddly-shaped grips, ropes, and rings. If you miss, you fall two-stories, splash into the ice-cold water below, red buzzers ignite, sirens sound, and millions upon millions of people watch you pick your soggy, failure-soaked self out of the pool as it's broadcast around the globe. You fail in front of a packed audience, TV cameras to the world, and then your fail lives immortality for all of the internet.

My journey started as a host, not a competitor. NBC hired me to host a series where I was this goofy, athletic guy catapulted into the heart of this incredibly intense and ambitious sport. I gave behind the scene exclusives, interviewed the top athletes, and even tried the most dynamic (that means difficult) new obstacles. The idea was that I'd give it a hearty attempt and probably fail hilariously. And I succeeded! Well, I succeeded…at failing. I failed a lot. Over and over again. I failed on these obstacles—these towering, gorgeous, imposing, monstrous, behemoths that rise two stories into the air. The first time I went on one, I actually ran out of breath just getting up to it. I could barely climb onto the obstacle that I was then supposed to fail. Do you know how humbling it is to fail *before you fail*? I was afraid of heights too, so when I finally got up there, I was trying not to blackout from being thirty feet in the air, while every wobble turned my stomach upside down, and my internal voice was racing: "Oh wow, this is high! Don't look down. Okay, you're looking down. Stop looking down, starting…now! Well, that didn't work." I had to summon all my strength to focus up so that I could give my best—to then, of course, fail. That first season, I failed on every single obstacle I touched. Every. Single. One.

Mind you again, these were not private failings. We were in the middle of a city—like Philadelphia, Indianapolis, or Los Angeles—and in front of live audiences. The *American Ninja Warrior* competitors and producers were all standing around watching. More cameras than you can count were positioned to catch every angle of my fails (in glorious HD!). And then there were the millions of viewers who would watch the series. I've failed on countless obstacles, in numerous cities, in front of millions of people. You could probably crunch the exact numbers, but it's **millions**.

That was our first season doing the series. I was asked to fail, and I nailed it. So even though the failings were a little embarrassing, they were still funny, and I was having a good laugh at myself too—and all the while falling deeply in love with this dream job, this community, and what *American Ninja Warrior* stands for in the world.

Enter Season Two. My bosses, the producers, came to me and said, "Alex, you are crushing it with failing!"

Blushing, I responded, "C'mon, thank you. Just doing my best."

They continued, "What if, for Season Two, you became good at this?"

Hmm. Bold idea. "This sport that Olympic gymnasts struggle to do?" I asked, as they nodded yes. "Well then...let's do it."

I knew how intimidated I felt (very!), but I also loved this job so much. The producers and creators of this series are incredible, and they've brought to life a sport that lifts people up, positively challenges them, and encourages us all to reach beyond our limits. And they asked me to be a public figure for this again—how cool! So even though I was scared and failed so many times before, I decided to believe in myself, give it everything I had, and...

I FAILED SOME MORE!!

Flung off obstacles, falling two stories, splashing into cold water, failing in front of millions of people live and immortally on the internet—just as I had in the first season. The critical difference now was that my bosses had asked me to perform better. They wanted me to succeed on the course—and that meant my *fun* failures were now *real* failures. My job description changed, and with those new expectations, I was not meeting my marks and I was scared.

> **Have you ever felt like you're not good enough? It's a horrible feeling.**

It feels like profound rejection and helplessness all stirred into a miserable cocktail, then topped off with a garnish of self-loathing. What was especially tearing me up was that I still had an opportunity. I had a chance to change it. I had a chance to become good enough, not to be helpless, not to be rejected, not to hate parts of myself—but I didn't know if I could do it, and that hurt even more.

I remember so vividly being in the hotel room after filming. The beds were perfectly comfy, but I couldn't sleep. I'd be up, staring at the ceiling, sick to my stomach with that deep nauseous feeling you get in the pit of your gut when every worst-case scenario is brought to life. *What if I keep failing? What if I get fired from my dream job? What if I lose my confidence, and then my career, and then my home, and then my friends, and I bet dogs on the street won't even come up to say hi anymore either!*

For all of us, there exists a moment where we take a big knockdown, and we might just stay down and stop. Back away from our goal while we allow our negative voice of fear to convince us that it's okay to give up—it's okay to give up on ourselves, give up on our goals, and give up on the people who need us. No. That is never okay and will never be okay for you. In this moment, we can either stay down or bounce back to our feet. But how do we jump back up?

That night in the hotel room, I zoomed out and thought about my life. Not my immediate, current, in-my-face life. But *life*. I then asked myself, "Alex, who do you want to be? What do you want for your moments of life?" (These are questions, by the way, that you and I are going to be exploring together in this book!) I thought about how much I loved this job, how much it meant to me, and that even though I was scared, I still had an opportunity to do something about it. There was so much out of my control, but I could still choose to believe in myself, give my best, and no matter what the results may be, at least I'd know that I didn't quit on myself. I wouldn't have to live with the gnawing pain of "what if" regrets. I pictured myself decades in the future with gray hair (the salt and pepper looks good by the way, not great, but good!). I'm going to look back on this right now and the real me, the bravely honest me in my heart of hearts, is going to know one truth: I either gave up on myself, or I gave this everything I had.

Right now, in your life, is there something that the negative voice of fear is trying to persuade you to give up on? Maybe it's an ambitious goal, a new habit, or building an important relationship. What if instead of giving into that voice and giving up on yourself—you give it everything you have with big, bold, positive action?

Late that night, while still staring up at the stucco white hotel ceiling, I made the decision to not listen to the negative voice of fear, and instead, take big, bold, positive action. I wondered, "What can I do that will make this daunting goal become possible?" A thought came to me, and part of me was hesitant to admit it, because the answer itself was so scary. The answer was: train with the best *American Ninja Warrior* competitors. If I want to be good at this sport, well, then do what the people who are good at it do. Even though that was deeply intimidating and, frankly, frightening, I knew it's what I needed to do to commit to myself. So, I jumped in the deep end. And let me tell you…it was intimidating! Frightening? Affirmative. Embarrassing? Yup. Frustrating? Oh, you betcha! But, *I was a part of it now*. There was no more canyon between me and this goal I had for myself. There was no more mysterious separation for my fear and doubt to breed. I couldn't hang on a monkey bar to save my life, but at least I was in the middle of the action. I was doing it. My goal had become real, and I was on the road to achieving it—even if it was a rocky road.

> **To this day, diving in the deep end—regardless of results, judgments, or even looking silly—is the biggest express route to reaching your goals.**

Now, as I started training with the elite *American Ninja Warrior* competitors, I quickly discovered that even though the physical demands were monumental, that was only part of the puzzle. I also needed to unlearn some beliefs about myself. You see, I'd failed so many times on so many obstacles that there was this false belief in me that I would always fail. Factually, that's what my track record had shown me too. But the biggest obstacle to overcome was not outside of me, but inside of me. I needed to prove to myself that "I always fail" was a lie.

> *I needed to prove to myself that "I always fail" was a lie.*

Is there a false belief about yourself, your life, or what you're capable of, that might just be a lie? Don't worry, we're going to call that lie out together. In this book, we're going to question some things! Fears, doubts, nerves, stress, anxiety, and uncertainties are all persuasive with their concerns, but they are opinions. Not facts. Opinions, not facts. Maybe some of those opinions are said with a lot of emphasis or volume—but they're still just opinions. And maybe, just maybe, the scared part of your brain is telling you lies.

You're not alone. I've had to navigate through that negative, fearful voice in my head a ton. During this time when I was proving myself as a host for NBC and digging deep to train with top American Ninja Warriors, I was also stepping into another dream of mine: becoming a professional speaker. There was no better way to

> *maybe, just maybe, the scared part of your brain is telling you lies.*

earn my keep as a professional speaker on Leadership and Peak Performance than to become an American Ninja Warrior, leading myself back from one of the toughest failures of my life. So that's exactly what I did.

And that's exactly what I'm going to give to you in this book. The lessons, tools, and strategies that elevated my work, my relationships, and my life. This Fail Proof System transformed me into an award-winning entertainer for NBC, a competitor *succeeding* on the *American Ninja Warrior* course, and an in-demand keynote speaker on stages around the world helping people become unstoppable.

Wherever you are right now; if you want to achieve record-breaking success, bounce back from a heartbreaking blow, or become an incredible leader for yourself and the people who need you—then you're in the right place. This system will do it for you.

| **You can accomplish anything in this world if you know *how* to fail. This book is the *how*.** |

Fail Proof Keys:

» Your negative voice of fear will try to convince you to quit on your goals and quit on yourself. Right now, is there anything it's trying to persuade you to give up on?

» What if instead of giving up, you give it everything you have with big, bold, positive action? Regardless of the result, you will be honoring a commitment to yourself.

» You can do anything in this world if you know *how* to fail.

How To Become Fail Proof

- - - - - - - - - - - - - - - - - -

*"If you're afraid to fail, you will never do the
things you are capable of doing."*
—John Wooden, Ten-Time NCAA Championship Coach

I've tried, tested, and experimented with all different strategies, lessons, takeaways, tools, hacks, and tactics for getting
to where you want to go. This book here is the clean manual
delivered right to you, without all the scrapes, scars, and sweat
I put in to figure it out. And I'm talking about literal scrapes,
scars, and sweat!

It took the visceral, in-your-face, high-repetition, and
high-octane failings with *American Ninja Warrior* to make
this system so clear to me, but I realized that I've called upon
this system in every defining chapter of my life to overcome
challenges and reach success.

I relied on it when I was struggling with insecurities, lack
of confidence, and fear of judgment all while speaking in front

of twenty thousand people live; as a competitor on *American Ninja Warrior* needing to overcome one of the hardest, and most public, failings of my life; and stepping up as a leader for the people who needed me, even when I was uncertain and unsure if I could do it. Like leading a championship team, and also being there for someone I love when they got sick. This system has helped me deeply, and I'm so deeply excited for it to help you, too.

The Fail Proof System is broken up into 6 Steps to unlock your goals, your leadership, and your life. Here is a bird's eye breakdown. As you're reading this glorious bald eagle view, if your mind pops up with certain goals, challenges, or fears, take note of them. That's it, just be aware of what comes up for you, and together we will embrace each one through this book.

The first step is claiming bravely honest goals—goals that actually matter to you. So much of modern life doesn't matter, and yet it steals away our time, energy, and focus. It steals our heartbeats. We're going to engage your self-awareness and self-navigation to get clear on what success really looks like to you, and why you want it. To do that, we need to explore, and I love the word *explore* because it's not judgmental. We live in a time where we judge everything. Everything is the best or the worst, the smartest or the dumbest, the right way or the wrong way. So often, we'll think of an idea or a goal, and our fear will quickly chirp up to tell us that it's unrealistic, impractical, or flat out just won't happen. It's going to take too much effort to do it, you're not skilled enough to do it, or it's simply impossible for you. Now, sometimes that fear voice comes from other people, and sometimes it comes from between our own ears. In fact, research shows the majority of our thoughts are negative.[2] Aren't brains fun?

I also love the word *explore* because it grants you freedom to imagine, experiment, fantasize, innovate, brainstorm, and create without fear's incessant judgments. Whether you are leading yourself or leading a group, allow time to explore. Pack some trail mix and go full Marco Polo. I've also intentionally used the word *claim* when talking about your goals. I know I've wrestled a lot in my life with the idea of deserving. Has that ever happened to you? You think of a goal, and part of you barks out, "Why do you deserve that? You don't!" By claiming your goals, you are not only setting them with purpose, but you are communicating to yourself that you do in fact deserve this goal. Claim your goals!

The second step is how you get started—accepting that there will always be factors outside of your control that impact your success, fulfillment, and well-being. But there are also very powerful factors within your control.

So, what can you get on your hands on? What can you touch in this moment to make your goal *real*?

Especially those meaningful steps that stretch your comfort zone. This is no easy feat, but there are ways to ignite a positive start and build momentum right away. Too often, goals die because they haven't been given their true shot to grow.

Once you've claimed your goal and kickstarted your momentum, Step 3 is about diving in, no matter how ugly, incomplete, or imperfect it looks. Whether it's an elegant swan dive or a gross belly flop that leaves your tummy

> *Too often, goals die because they haven't been given their true shot to grow.*

stinging and red, all that matters right now is that you get in the pool! Jump in the deep end. Even if it's overwhelming or humbling, you are now in the action and you will be surrounding yourself with elements that lift you up, make you better, and lead you toward your goal. This is huge!

Step 4 is how you kick in to hyperdrive. Failing is a process. It's a process of growing, learning, and improving—and it's an *emotional* process too. People give up because they want instantaneous achievement, and when it doesn't happen, our fear springs into action, "I told you! See? We'll never be able to do this, let's stop." No, fear, you stop! Good things take time, but time is the biggest variable of them all. I'm here so that you don't lose time. Some people hit resistance, and it takes them days to get over it. Or maybe weeks. There are some people who try to do something, it doesn't go well, and they never do that thing again. Worse, they convince themselves that they're not capable of it.

> **Hear me good and hear me now: you can do anything in this world if you know how to fail.**

Now what if you could expedite this process? What if you could go hyper speed? Step 4 begins the hyperdrive by giving you the tools to manage one of human beings' most volatile and unpredictable forces: emotions. Emotions can either be positive fuel or a sabotage of your success. Let's give you control over your emotions, so your emotions don't control you.

Now, failing is a process of growing, learning, and improving; but Step 5 is about *how* you actually grow, learn, and improve. So often people will summon determination to stick with a goal, but their results are not getting any better because they are missing the hidden clues to growth. Their enthusiasm for the goal then dies out—and the goal dies with it. But not for you. You will continually upgrade and elevate your performance because I'll show you how to uncover the hidden clues.

And finally, Step 6 is all about commitment. Commitment to yourself and the people who need you. How you keep dedicated to what you really want for yourself even in those moments of being struck down. Those moments when you've built up your momentum, you're beaming with confidence, you've hit your stride—and then life smacks you to the ground, knocks the wind out of you, and steals your favorite shoes.

When you laid it all on the line, and it wasn't enough; when you lose someone you thought you'd be with forever; when your industry shifts, your company changes, and your career is derailed; how do you bounce back then?

These are the make-or-break moments. To quote the movie *Tin Cup*, "When a defining moment comes along, you define the moment...or the moment defines you." We all want to close deals, win awards, and have a life bursting with love and happiness that we post up on social media for a ton of likes. But the seeds of achievement are rooted in the depths of these lows, and I will show you how to use them as your firepower. Most people will back away or halt in their tracks. But not you. You will be unstoppable.

We're going to dial up your confidence as well. Confidence can be an elusive currency, and I will give you my keys to building up your Confidence Bank—your inarguable, factual evidence to prove fear wrong—even when the funds seem low. We'll also make sure you are living a full and enriching life while we're making these goals happen.

> **There are too many cautionary cases of people who sacrificed the quality of their lives for misguided goals, only to realize what they lost too late.**

You nail the deal, but your home life is crumbling. You're taking care of others, but you're not taking care of yourself. You settle for a safe plateau in your career, but you know that you could step up to lead yourself and others to more. There are so many gifts in the fullness of this life, and I want them all for you.

Being unstoppable is also about loving your life. Life is unpromised, and to only look at the end goals while sacrificing the moments in between is tragic. All of the moments of your life, the impactful ones, the seemingly unimportant ones, the blissful ones, the horrible ones, the weird ones, the confusing ones—these moments of your life become your life. What if you didn't endure any of them, but you could embrace all of them? What if you could fall in love with all of these moments? What if you could fall in love with what you are doing, who you are becoming, and what you are leading? What if you could fall in love with your life?

> **What if you could fall in love with your life?**

That's what this Fail Proof System is here to do for you.

This system will be here for you in your highest highs, your lowest lows, and every moment in between. In work, relationships, and in life. This book will unlock your life, just like it did for mine. I know that it will do it for you, because I've seen it happen for everyone I share it with.

My greatest joy in this world is making people unstoppable. It's why I love being a keynote speaker for organizations, conferences, companies, and leaders around the world. Being able to witness the moment it clicks for people and seeing how it unlocks their lives is why I do what I do. Whether it's CEOs telling me that it's objectively increased their results, leadership, and performance; or individuals pulling me aside to let me know of the tough moments they've overcome and how now they've been able to reach their highest goals. It's beautiful, powerful, and makes my heart want to burst. I save every single letter, social media post, and message I receive from the people I've helped become unstoppable. I hope to someday get a card from you that talks about your huge successes, surrounded by amazing people that you love, while you truly and deeply feel proud and fulfilled by who you are. It will be a long card, but I've got a big fridge.

Fail Proof Keys:

» Pause your judgment, and give yourself a break to explore all of the wonderful possibilities for you and your life.

» Take notice of what emerges in your mind—the goals, the challenges, and the fears. Right now, the big win is just to be aware of them.

» The Fail Proof System is about achieving your goals *and* loving your life. Now is the time for your success, fulfillment, and well-being!

The Five Fail Proof Promises

_____

"You gain strength, courage and confidence by every experience in which you really stop to look fear in the face…. You must do the thing you think you cannot do."
—Eleanor Roosevelt, former First Lady of The United States

Okay, before we go any further, I need something from you. You're probably thinking, "Already?! Sheesh." I know, I know, but I need us to make a promise to one another. Well, *five* promises.

I'll go first: I promise you that I will be bravely honest with you about my highs, lows, and confusing times in between. I'll share my big, bold actions, both the swan dives and the belly flops. I promise to believe in you and your goals. I promise to give you the best of myself and everything I know, and I promise to be open to all the amazing gifts this journey together may bring us.

I promise you that, if you promise me this:

THE FIVE FAIL PROOF PROMISES

Be bravely honest. Be courageously truthful with yourself, your life, and what you want for it, even in the times when fear tries to deny it.

Take big, bold actions. Once you've decided to get in the pool of your goals, you're getting wet no matter if you dip your toes in or cannonball off the deep end. Big, bold actions yield big, bold results. Make a splash.

Choose to believe in yourself. Decide to believe in yourself even in the moments when your self-belief is tested. Always remember that this choice is in your power, and when you are presented with the option: choose to believe in yourself.

Give your best. At any moment, all you can do is the best you can do. No matter what is going on around you, you can always focus your energy to this truth: *"All you can do is the best you can do."* It's freeing, it's empowering, and it's got a nice ring to it too!

Be open to gifts. If you honor our promises, then you will receive so much more back than you could ever imagine. It will come to you in wonderfully different and beautiful ways from rewards to growth to amazing people, experiences, and opportunities too.

These are not half-hearted promises, though—you know, the kind you nod along with and then promptly forget. So, let's talk about what they are, what they mean, and how each promise is rooted in creating the Unstoppable You.

We'll start with the scariest: brave honesty.

BRAVE HONESTY

> **Bravery comes in many different forms. It's not always being big and loud, or with grand acts of heroism, or feats of strength. Bravery can happen in the quietest of times, when there's only two voices to be heard. The voice that is made up of fear, negativity, and uncertainty—and then the voice of the real you.**

Your heart, your soul, your true mind—not the one hijacked by fear. I call that real, true voice: your *positive energy* voice. It can be tempting to let that incessant, loud, negative voice win out. The tragic thing is that it's just trying to protect you. Fear is scared for you, so it wants to hold you back, or block your real desires from surfacing, because what if they don't work out? Then that will cause you pain. But denying what you want for yourself will cause much more pain than failing ever could. Here's the exciting thing: when you are bravely honest with yourself and set goals aligned with what matters most to you, that's when all the great things happen. That's when you tap into deeper levels of energy, passion, focus, creativity, and resourcefulness, because you really want to make this happen. It's the beating pulse of you being unstoppable, and it begins with brave honesty.

ACT BOLDLY

Doing, becoming, and leading the best we can is no easy feat. In fact, sometimes it's so daunting and overwhelming that it can feel like it's locked up away in this castle tower of "how could I ever?" It's even surrounded with walls of challenges, a thick fog of doubt, a moat of uncertainty, and guarded by a dragon who breathes fiery judgments. Each day, the fog grows thicker, and the tower grows a little bigger and seems to stretch farther away. You see, we can tend to build up our goals into these mythical pursuits, where they can be so intimidating, we don't even know how to start. But the key is just that—to start. And to start with big, bold actions! Why? Because you are going to tear down the mystery. It's like that classic scene in *The Wizard of Oz*, where Dorothy's little dog, Toto, pulls back the curtain to reveal that the big, scary Wizard isn't so big and scary after all—it was just the mystery that gave him false power. When we tear down the curtain on your huge, scary, mysterious goal, we find out it's actually just a series of do-able steps. More so, you've now *begun* the steps. You are in it. It doesn't matter if you did a swan dive, cannonball, or belly flop—you are now in the water, and you're swimming! You've also proven to yourself that you are capable of taking big steps, which will empower you to take the next step, and the next step. When you unlock this truth about yourself, you're on your way to becoming unstoppable.

CHOOSE TO BELIEVE IN YOURSELF

> **You may not have a choice about all things in life, but you will always have this one: to believe in yourself, or not.**

Now other factors are going to play into that, of course. How well you're performing, what other people think of you, heck, how well other people are doing around you. These are going to try to make the choice for you, but never forget that you carry a forcefield around this decision. The other factors may try to fire their lasers at it, and your negative voice will certainly poke at it as well, but you have the control. You have the power to make this choice, and when you are presented with it, over and over again, choose to firmly stand with yourself. When you do, you will have a deep peace and strength that comes with knowing you are dedicated to you—and it builds. You'll begin to see that commitment to yourself show up more and more across all areas of your life. Your forcefield of self-belief will grow stronger and stronger until it doesn't matter the size of anybody else's laser, or what is happening around you, or even the pokes from that negative voice inside of you. Right now, decide to honor yourself with this promise.

GIVE YOUR BEST

In any moment, all you can do is the best you can do. I will say that many times throughout this book because it's true, it's freeing, and it's empowering. And I hope it may just get stuck in your head like an inspirational jingle. It's so critical, because even before you've finished this book and become unstoppable, you will be presented with a moment where you need to put yourself out there, even though you don't know how it will go. In that moment, your mind may play a highlight reel of all the potential pitfalls, but just re-focus back to this central truth: all you can do is the best you can do. If you fully commit to giving your best without exception, I guarantee you will do better than the version of you who is held back because of doubts. Moreover, you are instilling an ever-growing trust in your ability to perform in the moments when you need it most, and when people need you the most.

> **What if you always did your best? In this moment. And this moment. And this moment. Before long, your life will be bursting at the seams with your best moments.**

Just think of how that might look over time in your work, in your relationships, and in your life. All you can do is the best you can do.

BE OPEN TO GIFTS

Life gives you gifts. Sometimes when you aren't aligned with what you really want, then you don't really care for the gifts. It's like receiving a gift certificate to the dentist. "A free fluoride treatment? Cool, yeah, I don't want this…" But when we are aligned, when we have set goals with brave honesty, choose to believe in ourselves, take bold actions, and give our best, well, then the gifts will be more beautiful, enriching, and rewarding than we could have ever guessed. As you put this Fail Proof System into your life, you will be both encouraged and excited about your growth. You're going to develop relationships that you never expected with people who truly want you to succeed. You will have experiences that are going to add layers and depth to your life, and you will unlock opportunities that you couldn't have imagined for yourself and the people who depend on you. In this fifth and final promise, you just need to be open to them. Open to seeing the gifts, allowing them to come into your life, and accepting them when they do. Then, simply be grateful for the gifts, feel the positive energy, and use it to keep being unstoppable.

These promises sit at the heart of everything we'll be doing in this book. They will be your foundation for a more fulfilling, joyful, and successful life.

So, let's do this again. I promise you that I will be bravely honest with you about my highs, lows, and confusing times in between. I'll share the big, bold actions I took (the swan dives and the belly flops). I promise to believe in you and your goals. I promise to give you the best of myself and everything I know, and I promise to be open to all the amazing gifts this journey together may give us. Now it's your turn.

THE FIVE FAIL PROOF PROMISES

Be bravely honest.

Take big, bold action.

Choose to believe in yourself.

Give your best.

Be open to gifts.

I'm imagining you saying these all out loud (you sound great!), and I'm choosing to believe that you will make these promises with me. So, do we have a deal? Thank you. More importantly, thank yourself! Because nothing will be impossible for you from this day forward. You are about to be unstoppable.

Ready? Then, let's begin.

Fail Proof Keys:
» Honor our 5 Fail Proof Promises together.
» You do not need to be perfect. We are the result of what we do *most often*. If you slip up, just come right back to the promises!

THE FAIL PROOF FUNDAMENTALS

What Is Failing? Reframing Failure & Leadership

"Failure is success in progress."
—Albert Einstein, Theoretical Physicist

You will fail. "Worst book ever!" I know, I know. But we all face failing, just not everyone knows *how* to fail. So to start, what is failure, anyway?

> **As a society we have a pretty screwed-up understanding of what it means to fail. As a result, we've endured unnecessary embarrassment, discouragement, shame, dread, and judgment that cuts us deep.**

We've cried, berated ourselves, maybe even thrown something. We've given up on lofty goals and, worst of all, convinced ourselves to give up *on ourselves*. To heck with that! My promise to you is that if you take the Fail Proof System to heart, you will never quit on yourself, never quit on your goals, and all of your experiences leading up to your goals will be more productive, fulfilling, and enjoyable.

SO, WHAT IS FAILURE?

Here's the short answer to that question: anytime an expectation doesn't match the reality. More specifically, failing is the gap between the result we expected and the result in reality. There's a fantastic scene in the movie *500 Days of Summer* in which Tom, played by Joseph Gordon-Levitt, gets invited to a party to see his ex-girlfriend-slash-love-of-his-life, Summer (played by Zooey Deschanel). As he steps into Summer's apartment, the movie goes split-screen: on the left, you see his expectation of how the night would go, and on the right, the cold, hard reality. On the expectation side, Tom reignites the romantic connection with the love of his life, and the two steal off to the corner of her roof completely absorbed in a romantic, magical reunion. On the reality side, you see Tom sitting in the corner, alone, ignored, and gazing over to see the woman he loves, blissfully showing off her new engagement ring. This disparity of expected result to real result is the foundation of failing—and it can sting.

Sometimes these gaps are big and grand and in your face. We expected career-high success, and we got fired. We expected our relationship to go on forever, and it ended. We thought we'd become someone else, and we didn't. Those are big, dramatic, and they hit hard, but our lives are filled with these micro-fails too.

Maybe you expected you'd get that project done by Friday. Or that your colleague would email you back the info you need. Maybe you thought a small disagreement with your partner wouldn't escalate into a fight. You might have assumed you were in better shape and that running three miles would hurt way less! You might even just expect a peaceful morning, but instead, your phone buzzes with a needless notification, you get distracted, and stub your pinky toe, which is a useless appendage but somehow hurts like the dickens.

There's a gap. We call that gap a failure, and we all face it. I don't think anyone is exempt from these moments. Maybe Beyoncé? Or Tom Brady? Maybe The Rock? (Probably The Rock.)

No way. I bet The Rock stubs his toe; he's huge. I bet Beyoncé gets in arguments, and I know Tom Brady has lost games. But they don't let those fails, setbacks, frustrations, and aching appendages stop them, do they?

You see, within these fails, there is unique opportunity—opportunity that most people don't see, and even if they do, they lack the knowledge, poise, and capability to do anything about it,

and so they're swept away in the downstream current of the fail until they eventually give up. They stop.

A fail only becomes a failure when you stop. Or when you allow the setback to spiral. The missed project turns into a lost job. The rough run turns into a month of skipped workouts. The stubbed toe makes you smack the table, hurting your hand, and knocking over your

> *A fail only becomes a failure when you stop.*

favorite mug which shatters to the ground. But if you seize this unique opportunity to improve and keep going, then that fail becomes failing. Failing is an active verb; it's progress. **Failing is the process of growing, learning, improving, and embracing possibilities!**

Think about the power of that perspective shift. Fails are steps in the process. You're not screwing up; you're learning! You don't suck; you're improving! Failing is going forward, it is moving ahead—if you know *how* to fail.

So how do we fail? All you need to do right now is identify moments in your life where expectation does not meet reality. In your work, in your relationships, and in your life. When you do, pause. Stop the downstream current. Don't let a bad minute become a bad day. Don't let a miscommunication become a falling out. Don't let a negative thought derail your ambition. Build that muscle of awareness right now. If you do that, you are creating opportunities for yourself that most people miss. And in the chapters ahead, I will show you how to not only seize these opportunities but maximize their potential for you.

REFRAMING LEADERSHIP

Leadership is a term that can sometimes feel sterile, cold, or even impersonal. Like we need to be this perfect model of brilliant decision-making, courageous action, and electric confidence. Now those are all great, but I'd like to give you a leadership reframe.

Leadership is caring about people: knowing where they are, where they want to be, and getting them there.

When you look closer at that definition, you may notice something—it has nothing to do with job descriptions. That's because you can be a leader in any area of your life, and I'm here to tell you that you are a leader, whether you realize it or not. People need you. Anytime you can care about someone, and support them from where they are to where they want to be—well, X marks the spot, you're a leader!

So when it comes to the people in your life—whether in work or relationships—where are they right now? How are they doing? Any challenges they're facing?

Ask them.

Where do they want to go? What are their goals? How can we align those goals with our goals so we are truly on the same team?

Ask them.

And then help them get to their goals. Support and challenge people to push past their limits and reach levels that maybe they weren't even sure they could reach. It begins with caring about them. Genuinely caring. Not "caring" with a gift card. But caring about the human being. You don't need to be best buds, in fact, that might not be the healthiest dynamic anyways. But you do need to connect with them and foster a bond so that you genuinely care about leading them to success. Anybody who fakes caring can only pretend for a little while, and it's only a matter of time before they lead their people and their organizations astray.

> **Here's the quick and easy hack to caring about people: don't pretend to care about people. Actually *care* about people.**

Now what's incredible about this system is as you notice these fail moments in your own life and course correct back on track, you'll also be able to identify it for the people around you, and you can step in to be that shift for them. This is how you truly become an impactful leader, and also one who shows you care about your people. If Brian missed closing a deal, instead of shaming him and derailing him further, you can step in to find out why he is struggling and support him to do better. You've now not only improved performance and results, you've shown Brian that you care about Brian. And you've shown your organization that you care about people. Maybe you'll even set the example for your culture to be one that cares about people too. How 'bout that.

Fail Proof Keys:
» A fail only becomes a failure when you stop.
» Failing is the process of growing, learning, improving, and embracing possibilities! Let's release the unnecessary and harmful shame around it.
» Catch moments in your life where your expectation doesn't meet reality—and don't let it sweep you downstream.
» Leadership is caring about people: knowing where they are, where they want to be, and getting them there. And you are a leader in all areas of your life.

5

Your Self-Belief: What Do You Believe About You?

"The real difficulty is to overcome how you think about yourself."
—Maya Angelou, Poet

Have you ever ice-skated in wooden clogs?

I hope not. It's a terrible idea. It can be hard enough to stay upright on ice while you're wearing ice skates. Fashion preferences aside, wooden clogs are probably the worst footwear for performance. They're clunky, heavy, and hard to maneuver even on a smooth, dry sidewalk; not to mention skating on slick ice. It's probably why clogs are rarely a favorite of speed skaters.

And yet that feeling—slipping and sliding, while also feeling heavy and weighed down—I've felt that before, and I'm sure you have, too. That's what it feels like when we get sucked into the vortex of busyness, false productivity, pressures, and scrambling to satisfy other people's demands. You're clambering to go forward but also fighting to stay upright. You're moving a lot but not going anywhere, burning your energy for no gain. Ice skating with wooden clogs. **Wouldn't you rather have a pair of skates?**

Before we get into all the practical ways to make you unstoppable, we've got to do a deep dive into, well, YOU.

| **All meaningful results and rewards start inside of you.**

External growth and transformation begin with internal growth and transformation, and it's impossible to do it the other way around. That's how massively important your inner life is to your outward life, specifically, what you believe about yourself and how you speak to yourself. Everything builds from there.

In this book, you will get all the real-world, actionable steps for bringing your goals to life for yourself and the people who depend on you. But first, we need to make sure that we build you a solid internal foundation, brimming with strength and positive energy to power you ahead. So that's where we'll start, because there's no sense in teaching you to speed skate until you take off those darn clogs.

WE ALL SPILL COFFEE

Do you ever feel like you are your own worst critic? I spilled my coffee this morning and blurted out: "Well, that was stupid, wasn't it?" So, not only did I scold myself, but I also apparently felt the need to ask myself to concur on my stupidity. And what was my fatal sin? Spilling coffee. A little intense, no? Have you ever done something like that?

Maybe it's not a coffee spill that gets you, but we all have our thing. My buddy Matt loses it at himself when he misses his exit on the freeway. Alicia, one of the athletes I train with, refuses to take pointers from the rest of us when she's frustrated; she will just go to the corner as if she sent herself to timeout. I consulted a CEO who used to, like clockwork, call me ten minutes before his big meetings to tell me all his ideas are "trash," he's "garbage," and the meeting is going to be a "dumpster fire of trash and garbage." (His words, not mine.) It didn't matter how nice his suit was, he was firmly wearing wooden clogs to those meetings. These might sound like unique quirks, but we all have them. I've lost mornings to cruddy moods that stemmed from a few spilled drops of medium roast. Matt has banged up his car because he wasn't paying attention after missing his exits. Alicia wastes entire training sessions repeating the same mistake. And if we didn't course correct the CEO's mindset, the mini-meltdowns would have snowballed into full-fledged meltdowns and been a wrecking ball into the meeting and everything thereafter. It's like something takes over our brains and completely derails us—and that's because something is.

We all have this inner voice that seems like it's eagerly waiting to take us down a peg—like a wild jungle cat stalking out its prey. But we are the jungle cat *and* we are the prey! We're attacking ourselves. These little "quirks" end up mushrooming **We're attacking ourselves.** into larger, more in-your-face problems—because they're not quirks. They're deeply rooted and malicious beliefs about ourselves.

The reality of our experience as human beings is that we have a propensity to being negative. In fact, a study from the University of Pennsylvania shows that our negative thoughts are both more potent and contagious than our positive ones.[3] More potent *and* contagious. Well, jeez, that's not ideal. The negativity is like an oil spill in our minds, toxic and damaging. I've found the real trouble is not in vague negativity, but accurate negativity. Meaning, let's say you have a specific doubt or concern about yourself, like speaking in front of groups. If your negative voice simply said you were horrible at banjo, I doubt that would have a strong impact on you (banjo fanatics aside). But what if your negative voice told you that you're horrible at public speaking right before you presented in front of your organization. Now let's say that presentation didn't go perfectly, and there were mess ups. Your negative voice is going to jump right on it with arms waving, flagrantly pointing to those mistakes as the validation of all your concerns. "See, I was right! I told you that you're not good at this, and here's the proof. I found it!" It's like a little kid celebrating after finding an Easter egg, except it's inside your mind and it's celebrating your deepest concerns. It's far less fun and with much fewer jelly beans.

In this example, the negative voice of fear is harming us in three distinct, dangerous, and sneaky ways. First, if you've ever been about to do something important, and then have your brain feel like it turns against you, it's a horrible thing to experience. "Stupid, backstabbing brain!" Second, it's actually sabotaging your performance. Even if you don't indulge fear's persuasive opinions, you are still distracting your focus away from the task at hand right as it's about to happen. If you're about to meet with a client, or kick off a pitch, or finally tackle the new workout challenge, the last thing you want to do is have to perform well AND debate your inner voice. Lastly, and quite possibly the most important of all, is that

| **consistently believing your negative voice of fear can actually harm your body and shorten your life.** |

Research from Molecular Biologist and 2009 Nobel Prize Winner, Dr. Elizabeth Blackburn, shows that increased periods of this pessimistic state can cause your cortisol level to rise, damage your DNA, and increase your risk for illnesses.[4]

So, why is your brain doing this? And even more important, how can you change it?

EVERYTHING OUTSIDE OF YOU BEGINS WITHIN YOU

Our powerful beliefs are the driving force behind our thoughts, words, and actions. What you believe about yourself will show up in your life. This is because you will think, speak, and act in line with the person you believe you are.

Meaning, if you believe you are phenomenal at your job, you will think, speak, and act like someone who deserves a promotion. If you believe you are a fraud at your job and it's just a matter of time before your boss fires you, then you are going to think, speak, and act like someone who deserves to get canned, whether you want to or not.

On the other hand, what's exciting about this is that if you believe you are a fantastic friend, or a genius capable of solving your company's problems, or that you love yourself and are committed to improving your life—or all of the above, while also feeling gorgeous and like your body is a ten out of ten—well, imagine what might happen.

Let's put this into a practical example. If you believe you are healthy and in terrific shape, your behavior will resemble it. Because you believe you are fit, it will be much smoother for you to be active, eat healthy, and feel like a fit version of yourself. That's your operating system, so that's how your program will run. You may even start to look forward to hitting that workout class or enjoy drinking that green veggie-omega-flax seed smoothie. As you do, you'll see and feel yourself becoming more fit (hey hey!) which will validate your internal belief and spur you to keep making it true. External results are the product of internal beliefs. The same thing goes, though, if you believe you are a lazy bum. You will be more likely to act sluggish, eat poorly, and overall, just feel worse about yourself. That's in-line with the belief. Now, you can certainly feel like a lazy bum at times and passionately use it as motivation to get in better shape. That's positive fuel. But if your consistent self-belief is pounding you over and over again that you are a lazy bum, then you will keep acting like it and nothing will change. Right now in your life, are there any destructive beliefs that could maybe use an update?

> **External results are the product of internal beliefs.**

I've certainly felt this at times in my life. After completing Division I college lacrosse, a deep dream of mine, I stopped believing I was an athlete. I ate horribly, I wasn't working out, and I even quit engaging in activities that I loved (read: playing sports). I remember when I finally figured out that I had let myself go. I put on my favorite shirt, and I thought the dryer had shrunk it 3 sizes. The poor customer service folks at Whirlpool had to break the hard truth to me: I was very overweight. As someone whose identity has always been an athlete, this really made me feel like a failure. The kind Whirlpool rep didn't use the word lazy bum, but my head certainly did. I started feeling terrible about my body, my self-worth deteriorated, and my confidence plummeted with it. But here's a dangerous little factoid: my negative belief of "I'm not an athlete" didn't come from me. It came from other people telling me this, and I blindly accepted it as truth. They assumed this to be the case about my life, and I accepted their assumptions as facts. And that hurt me. Hear my plea: **do not blindly accept someone else's belief about you to be true**. I want to scream this in the town square while ringing a giant bell, "Hear ye, hear ye! Don't believe other people's beliefs about you! Just because Sam thinks you're not creative, doesn't mean you're not creative. Maybe Sam just sucks!" The first step to coming out of that "former athlete" phase was to believe that I was capable of being "an elite athlete in the best shape of my life." It was tough to fully believe this was possible while still being out of shape in that shrunken shirt, but that's exactly the importance of claiming our goals. It communicates to us that not only is it possible, but we are worthy of this goal, and it focuses our energy in its direction. Once I started to believe that it could be *possible*, that's when I became drawn to being more active, eating better, and ultimately changing my behavior to then change the results in my life. Results like becoming an athlete in the best shape of my life and competing on *American Ninja Warrior*, one of the most difficult physical challenges on earth.

Even now with *American Ninja Warrior* my beliefs about myself are tested often. Because of how hard it is, when I have a poor session, it can be so easy to want to believe that "I'm bad at this." I've had to become very mindful and realize, "No, that's not the case. I'm not bad just because this instance wasn't my best. I just need to use it as positive fuel to re-focus and commit." This is where we need to honor that promise of choosing to believe in ourselves. When positive beliefs are paired with positive actions, amazing things happen.

> When positive beliefs are paired with positive actions, amazing things happen.

If your self-belief is that you are getting in the best shape of your life, or that you're having your highest grossing year ever, or that you are deeply connected with the person you love, well, then your thoughts, words, and actions are going to get you there. This is not being delusional or convincing ourselves of a lie. It's quite the opposite. You are recalibrating your GPS to the destination you want for yourself. These small tweaks have big impacts. Rather than fixating on what you don't want, this targets our focus and positive energy to what you do want for yourself. Today, keep an observing eye over some of the beliefs that you have, and see if you can make these changes in perspective and language. It's critical and cannot be overlooked or ignored. We won't be perfect at it, and we don't need to be; all we need to do right now is identify these opportunities to shift our beliefs and start to course correct. It's like degrees on a map. If we alter even just a little in a positive way, then the results over time will be remarkable.

BELIEFS MEET BRAVE HONESTY

I come from New York, type A, "suck it up and do your job." So I can hear some people saying "enough with this beliefs malarky, get to the action!" We will. But I promise you that actions stem from beliefs. And if your beliefs are misguided and ineffective, then your actions and results will be misguided and ineffective too. We've talked a lot about brave honesty, and here's where it shows up in a big way. We need to be bravely honest with how we see ourselves, and most importantly, what you believe to be true about yourself. (PS, I love New York, and I miss good bagels.)

Let's zoom back to my spilled cup of coffee. There's more to that story that I need to share with you.

There have been plenty of times where I've scolded myself for spilling some coffee, but this most recent time was different. I did scold myself, but then I paused and laughed about this ridiculously over-the-top reaction. I then refocused on *why* I spilled my coffee.

Hmm. I spilled it because I was in a rush. I was rushing because I was late for a meeting. I was late for the meeting because I laid in bed for longer than usual. I laid in bed for longer than usual because when my alarm went off, I grabbed my phone, "accidentally" opened my email, and saw an update from a colleague who is absolutely killing it—and I felt worthless and stewed about it for ten minutes.

Ah. So, I spilled the coffee because I felt worthless. I was scrambling to become worthwhile, and that is why I knocked over the mug.

You may read this, and think "No, you spilled the coffee because you are clumsy." Well, thanks for that, and I do tend to bump into a lot of walls. But so often, we react to the surface-level results without digging at why they happen and where they come from. When we investigate with just a little brave honesty, we uncover a more meaningful—and correctable—explanation. Meaning, in this example, rather than frantically searching to be worthwhile, I can focus my energy on more solid, consistent sources of self-worth, doing things that actually make me feel worthwhile and less rocked by comparison. I could also refocus on being inspired and excited for my colleague, rather than feeling jealous. 7 a.m. is too early for jealousy anyways. We must dig to find the causes, not just look at the surface level effects.

A few years back, I presented a keynote for this international company, and a Swiss gentleman came up to me after and said, "You are a cause." I awkwardly paused as I partially thanked him, while also not really knowing if this was a compliment, if I misheard him, or if that's just a popular phrase in Zurich: *"Hey Suzie, you're a cause!"*

"Ummm…what?" I asked.

He responded, "There are causes and effects in this world. You are a cause." To this day, it's one of the most meaningful sentences I've ever been told.

> **There are causes and effects in this world. There are causes and effects in your life. *Be a cause*.**

If we bring this level of brave honesty not just to final effects and results—whether spilled coffee, or missed deals, or a shouting match with someone we love—but we dig at why they happened and the cause you are being, then that's when we have the power to change it. You have the power to focus your contribution to your life—your actions, words, and beliefs—on what will lead you to the results you desire.

This is big, because spilled coffee exists in all areas of our lives.

WHAT DO YOU BELIEVE ABOUT YOU?

"Whether you think you can, or you think you can't—you're right," said Henry Ford, the industry magnate who brought us the Ford automobile company and the Model T, the first widely owned vehicle in America. And I'll take his words one level further. Studies show we have 70,000 thoughts a day, and only 6,200 of those are conscious thoughts.[5]

This means that about 86 percent of our thoughts are on auto-pilot. But who's the auto-pilot? Your beliefs. Thoughts are a product of beliefs.

So, to further Mr. Ford's quote: If you *believe* you can, or you *believe* you can't—you're right. Who's in control of your beliefs? You. Meaning you can actively create and cultivate positive self-belief, no matter what else is going on.

Here are techniques to instill more positive self-beliefs right now, and recalibrate back to more positive states when you need to:

Reframe the Belief. Just like we are doing with reframing failure, can you reframe your negative beliefs? Meaning, let's say you think, "I hate my life." Pretty intense one, huh? Agreed, and let's see if we can do this practice with one of the toughest beliefs. Okay, so that belief passes through you. When it does, can you catch it, and then reframe it to "my life is improving every day"? We're not disagreeing with your initial sentiment that life is rough right now, but we are shifting your perspective and energy to a more positive direction. This is a muscle, and you will need to strengthen it by reinforcing this new belief often. Especially for those negative beliefs we've been carrying with us for a long time. Now what's beautiful is that as you pair that new positive belief with big, bold positive actions, then your life most certainly will improve. It may even improve to the point where you start to like your life, or quite possibly believe, "I love my life."

Moving to **Positive.** It can be difficult to switch from negative to positive. These early chapters exist to give you foundational tools, tactics, and techniques to rid fear and negativity from your life as much as possible. While you're developing that incredible foundation, you may also benefit right now from some quick-action solutions. Meaning, say you need to shift your mood...now! This is the biggest state switcher right here: get in your body. You are a physical creature of life. Go get some air, walk around, let the sun touch you, move to your favorite music, enjoy your favorite food, or simply close your eyes and experience a cycle of extended inhales and exhales. Even if we wear nice sweaters and use fancy words, we are all still living creatures, and this is the quickest hack into being more positive.

Realize Your Power. Here's what's exciting. We don't have jurisdiction over what other people do, say, or believe. Zero. Zilch. Nada. If we did, that would be sorcerer level wizardry, and we'd all have to get those big pointy top hats. But we do have ultimate jurisdiction over what *we* do, say, and believe. You have such control, in fact, that you alone can change them into being more positive and powerful. No one else has to co-sign on that, and it can happen any moment—like right now. You can quite literally be the writer of your story. Instead of beating ourselves down, we can lift ourselves up. So, what's your story?

WHAT STORY WOULD YOU LIKE TO WRITE?

There is a popular quote that says, "You are the main character of your story."

Now, I love the idea of us being the main characters in our stories. It feels whimsical like there may be a quest, or potions, maybe even a soundtrack when it's made into a movie. But the word *story* also implies conflict, struggle, and drama! Who wants to hear a story where everyone is happy and life is just peachy? Being the main character means we are at the whim of the story. The story is the driving force, and we are just playing a role in the saga.

What is more exciting than just being the main character is that you are the main character *and* the writer. You are creating the main character played by you (congrats on the role!). Now, to date, this main character of yours has been written by a lot of co-authors. You, of course, have had a meaningful writing credit, but I'd imagine parents, family, loved ones, good friends, not good friends, romantic partners, ex-romantic partners, bosses, colleagues, competitors, society, and your negative mind itself have all had substantial contributions too. What they've done and said has played a role in shaping your main character right now. You have no jurisdiction over their input and never will, but where you do have ultimate jurisdiction is over your actions, words, and beliefs about yourself. That is what's so critical, pivotal, and exciting.

What it means is that no matter what has contributed to your life, and no matter what may happen from this point on, you still have the final say in your actions, words, and beliefs—and that is what will drive everything that happens in your life. You have absolute authority, creative direction, and artistic design. You are not just the main character; you are the creator of your main character.

Now, let's add in a hearty dose of brave honesty and take a look at the main character that's been created up to this point. We need brave honesty because sometimes it can be tough to truly shine the spotlight on areas that don't match up with what we want for ourselves. So tough in fact, that we can block them out, compartmentalize them away, or even just ignore those dark corners all together. It takes bravery to accept the truth that maybe there is room for your main character to get a rewrite. If you're like me, then in your life, you've had some days of poor writing. You've made bad decisions, done things you regret, and missed chances you wish you took. Maybe you

> You are not just the main character; you are the creator of your main character.

had a skinny-jeans phase that caused you to walk like a toy soldier and even ripped open when you suddenly bent over to tie your shoe while in line at the juice bar. Just me? Don't shame yourself for any of the life steps and missteps that have created you right now, but instead be bravely honest, knowing that none of this is a life-sentence, and you are capable of changing anything in your story right now. Even if the store won't take back your ripped skinny jeans, and you have to find a new juice bar.

Here are questions to explore with brave honesty and not self-abuse. As you do, run it through your different stories: your work, your relationships, and your life.

. . . .

Who is your main character right now? Describe this character. *(In your work, in your relationships, and in your life)*

What is your main character good at? What isn't your character good at? *(In your work, in your relationships, and in your life)*

What do you believe is possible for you moving forward? *(In your work, in your relationships, and in your life)*

What do you believe is impossible for you? *(In your work, in your relationships, and in your life)*

One more question, and run it by each of your answers above:
Is this true?

. . . .

No, really. Is it true? Push back a little bit on your answers here and see if maybe we're taking something at face value that just might not be accurate. Or even if it is true, could that truth evolve and change to be better? For instance, if you believe you aren't funny, or you're not athletic, or you don't have the courage to take risks—could any of those beliefs be wrong? If you think you're not able to reach a new level of your career, or your relationship has lost its spark, or that you'll always wrestle with confidence—could any of those beliefs be false? If you believe you're too old, or not experienced enough, or don't have the resources or means or luck to make meaningful changes—might that be wrong? Maybe those are beliefs based off what someone else contributed to your story. Or maybe it's just based off a singular experience, and we're taking it is a hard fact, when it's not.

When it comes to what you said is impossible for you, is there any way that those impossibilities could become possibilities? Do you think that maybe, just maybe, none of this is set in stone and that you are capable of changing anything you want? Forget the "how"; I'm going to give you the "how."

All you need to do right now is choose to believe that all of this is possible for you. Because it is.

Choose to believe that you are worthy of being a main character who loves your work, loves your relationships, and loves your life. That's the story I want for you!

Now, let's get to writing it.

FOCUS ON YOUR *POSITIVE ENERGY* VOICE

The writing room of your life can be a tough place. There are a lot of voices jockeying to make their case. The negative, fearful voice. The positive, hopeful voice. And a chorus of other ones in between, all battling for your attention. It can sometimes feel like you're a substitute preschool teacher trying to manage this unruly bunch. You've got voices that are sweet and loving, ones that are whining or scared, ones that are throwing a tantrum, and then that one who seems lost and is just in the corner eating glue. But, you get to choose which one you listen to. You can have a favorite student, and I'd like to nominate your *Positive Energy* voice.

A few hours after my spilled coffee saga, I went off to train for *American Ninja Warrior*. I'm passionately positive with my fellow competitors. I find a deep joy in rooting them on and hyping them up. But when I, myself, made a mistake, what voice do you think wanted to pop in my head? Is it the voice of positive encouragement, like I'm treating myself as a dear friend? Or was it the scolding voice, reprimanding myself for making a mistake?

Remember, there is power in awareness. In recognizing that the voice telling us that we're a latte-spilling loser may not have our best interest at heart, and in fact is just voicing an opinion, not facts—a pretty lousy opinion if you ask me. We can then choose not to listen to that negative voice and instead choose to focus on the voice that better serves and supports us.

Right now, wherever you are and whatever time it is, think about your past day. Was there a moment that you scolded yourself? I don't mean "tough love" where you forced yourself to work out or made yourself hustle to meet a deadline—that's actual love and honoring our goals. No, I mean a time when you were unnecessarily brutal to yourself, even harassing and punishing yourself. How did it make you feel? What impact did it have on your situation? How might it have gone if you were positive, supportive, and cultivating of yourself instead? What if, in your head, the default voice wasn't one of negativity and fear, but of positive energy? Passionately and consistently getting your back, supporting you, challenging you with love, and powering you forward like your own personal 24/7 hype person? Imagine what you may be capable of doing, becoming, and leading.

Now, this next chapter will earn me a difficult conversation with someone I love, but I'm willing to do that to support you. I feel like I owe it to you. So, here we go.

Fail Proof Keys:

» You are not just the main character, you are the creator of your main character.

» Negative beliefs undermine you and sabotage your success—whether coming from someone else or coming from yourself.

» Right now in your life, are there any negative beliefs that could use an update? Spot them, and when you do, replace it with a more positive belief.

» When you pair positive beliefs with positive actions, amazing things happen.

Your Self-Talk: What Are You Saying To You?

"Talk to yourself like you would to someone you love."
—Brené Brown, Research Professor, and Bestselling Author

I can trace a lot of my negative beliefs and self-talk back to my upbringing. I love my dad very much. We have a unique relationship, and I'm thankful for it, but he's a tough guy. He is intense, and he can be very negative and unpredictable. A triple-threat, if you will. Growing up, when things went a little bad, they'd quickly escalate to the worst. I felt like I was always walking on thin ice (in clogs). I was scared to death that I'd disappoint him, that I'd fall short of his expectations. I was terrified of failing. Here's the thing: my dad is also incredibly supportive of me. I can't think of a single lacrosse game where he wasn't there in the bleachers. Or driving me to hockey tournaments hours away. Even chess tournaments. Yup, you heard that right. Everything is intense with my dad. I showed a little promise in chess, so next thing you know, I'm in chess tournaments. Gosh those were…interesting. You ever hear chess kids talking trash? "There goes your rook, sucker!"

My dad also used to be a math teacher, so every night we'd do my math homework together. He would severely sharpen three number two pencils before he'd tap his finger on the table, and that meant for me to take out my math homework and do it in front of him. When I would get a question wrong, he would erase it so vigorously that the paper would tear. My dad cared very much about me and wanted to support me. The support was just misguided at times and would show itself as incredible intensity. I know that he was scared of me failing. I'm his son, and what would happen to me if I failed out there in life? So, there was incredible intensity to perform well, and anything below 100 percent perfect was unacceptable and met with very strong words at a very strong volume. Misguided is the key word here, because it wasn't out of a lack of love or care or support for me. The intensity was just misguided. Instead of it being a babbling brook that gently floated me up, it was an explosive geyser.

I look back, and I realize that it was just his negative, fearful beliefs that were taking ownership of his love for me. The same negative beliefs that you and I both possess and that we all have the choice to either accept or dismiss.

Growing up, my fear of disappointing showed up in two drastically different ways. I would either go so hard at anything I did with immense intensity and nerves to be 100 percent perfect—or I would try to disappear entirely.

> **Most of my life had been one of those two extremes. Either desperately trying to prove myself, or desperately trying to shrink myself away.**

It hit its first peak when I was in junior high. I was much younger than my siblings because, well, I'm an Accident Kid; I know this because my older sister is six years older than me. My parents named her Alexis, and six years later, they named me Alex…pretty sure mistakes were made. So, when my siblings left home, I was in seventh grade and perpetually uncomfortable in my own skin, awkward and afraid to be my full self—which was super fun, because you know how easy it is in junior high to be yourself.

I believed that I was awkward, uncomfortable, unaccepted, and that I wasn't good enough to be liked by other people. And so, my thoughts, words, and actions reinforced that belief. I acted awkward, uncomfortable, unaccepted, and unworthy of a friendly invitation to the lunch table. I imagine the school bully was walking by and realized, "Oh hey, I'll just bully that kid. He's already playing the part!" And he did. Joey Lautner. I'll never forget him. (Joey, if you see this, please don't sue or take legal action; you owe me this.)

Joey would walk up to me in the halls and, as quick as a cobra strike, aggressively twist my, ahem, nipple region. And it hurt! It made me paranoid, walking the hallways with my hands clasped over the target area as my last line of defense. I looked like I was at a town pool trying to keep my bikini top from falling down. Spoiler alert: that's not a cool look to make new friends!

Joey wasn't my only bully either. It got so bad that I would eat lunch alone in the math room with my one buddy, Geoff.

Based off my dad's intensity, I became pretty darn good at math—go figure. It was a safe spot for me. I'd eat lunch there, because in the cafeteria, I would just get made fun of and beaten up. I think back to that thirteen-year-old me, and I feel for the little guy, because I remember how defeated, disengaged, and flat out sad I felt.

Then a leader came into my life. The high school lacrosse coach came and watched our middle school practice. He came over to me afterward, pulled me aside, and said, "Hey, I think you could be good at this. This could really be something in your life." Now that thirty-five-second conversation, which could have just as easily never happened, changed my life. Coach Paul Carcaterra forever deepened my appreciation of what leaders can do, and I'll forever be grateful to him for it.

As a leader, you can change a person's life. And you are capable of doing it in any moment. Remember that.

And fun fact, he's now a top TV analyst in the sport of lacrosse, further proof that caring about people leads to success.

Coach Carc (as he's epically known in the lacrosse world; he's helped a lot of athletes) gave me a purpose, a goal, a direction, and a dream—a real one, something I could visualize. Dreams can be anything. For you, it might be record-breaking revenue, a blissfully happy family, or being a leader in your organization. When the target becomes clear, the dream becomes *real*. My first *real* dream had to do with the sport of lacrosse. Coach Carc

When the target becomes clear, the dream becomes real.

gave me more than just a dream in sports. He gave me the gifts that come with our true goals. Like friends! Let's not get it confused here; I was an awkward, uncomfortable, bullied teen with no confidence, and all of a sudden, I have this outlet where the better I am, then the better my life. I became obsessed. Every day, I'd say to myself, "I am a High School All-American and Division I lacrosse player." I would tell myself this all the time. Walk by a mirror and, "Oh, look at that High School All-American and Division I lacrosse player." Catch my reflection in the car window and pop a quick bicep flex: "Hey there, you High School All-American and Division I lacrosse player." I'd wish it every chance I got, too. On every coin in a wishing well, or shooting star, or birthday candle—even if it wasn't my birthday. I'd just steal the cake from Grandma. "Sorry, Nana. This is for my dream!" I was doing this at the time because I was fixated, but what I didn't realize was that I was instilling positive self-talk and positive self-belief, which then quickly showed up in my behavior.

You see, in addition to high-fiving that High School All-American and Division I lacrosse player in the mirror, I was practicing lacrosse all the time. All of the time. With my team, in the backyard, even inside my house I would try to dodge past my poor mom while she was just trying to make dinner. I loved training, because it was aligned with my self-beliefs and self-talk. Going the extra mile was frictionless, because I really believed in myself to be on track for this goal. It was then reflected in the external results, and I achieved my dream goal. I was a High School All-American and went off to play Division I lacrosse in the Ivy League. But, here's one critical thing to note: I did achieve my dream goal, however I was still dealing with extreme nerves, lack of confidence, and a fear of failure. For a period, my positive obsession allowed my performance to override all these negative beliefs. But, only for a period.

Here's where my upbringing caught up to me.

At my core, I was still this kid who struggled with self-belief, who was brutally harsh with my self-talk and deeply scared of failing. So when I came into the Division I team, I was still the kid—albeit in a big body—who would either go so hard with severe intensity and nerves to be 100 percent perfect or try to disappear entirely. That inconsistency resulted in me starting every single game as a freshman *and* benched every single game the next year.

Fired. Lost my job on the team. Not just my job, but my lifelong dream. Even more than that, I lost my purpose, my identity, and my self-worth. I was devastated, and it rippled into all areas of my life, like that toxic oil spill. I lost my confidence in work, relationships, and my life. I started to struggle in school, I became distant with my friends, and my girlfriend and I broke up. Well, if we're splitting hairs, she broke up with me.

It was tearing me up inside, because it meant so much to me and had also given me so much. I loved the game, I loved my teammates, and I loved our organization; and now, because I couldn't stop my negative spirals, it all disappeared. I tried to depend on my performance abilities to power through as I had done in the past, but the heartbreaking truth was that there was nothing outside of me that could help me.

I remember after one game, it reached a breaking point, and I started to break down in the locker room. I didn't want my teammates to see, so I ran off to hide in the only place I could—a bathroom stall. I was sobbing in there, tucking up my legs to hide, while I choked down the tears into my jersey, because I didn't want my teammates to hear me. I will never forget that moment. It's the moment I let my negative voice win, and I lost my dream.

The next year, I came back and was one of the team's top scorers, but only out of sheer will and effort. I didn't heal anything. Even though I performed well here and there, I never enjoyed it, and I was still struggling on the inside because I was feeding myself nothing but negative self-talk.

Studies show that consistent negative self-talk has wildly destructive implications just like negative beliefs, which makes sense, since we will speak in-line with our beliefs. Negative self-talk can actually create mental health issues, decrease our performance, and skyrocket our stress. A lot of that stress is ironically self-inflicted. Elizabeth Scott of *Very Well Mind*, an online resource library, explains that those with negative self-talk are altering their reality to create an experience where they don't have the ability to reach the goals they've set for themselves.[6]

> **It's quite an unfortunate cycle: our negative self-talk limits our abilities to reach our goals, which in turn, causes more negative self-talk.**

The answer is replacing negative self-talk with positive self-talk—positive self-talk, which raises our confidence, energy, oxytocin, creativity, and vitality.

Well, great. But easier said than done, right? How do we do this, how do we heal ourselves? What if I were to tell you that you could heal yourself through healing others?

A few years after being the heartbroken nineteen-year-old crying in the bathroom stall, I started coaching high school lacrosse. What was fascinating was that I could see myself in the young men I was coaching. I understood how they were feeling when they missed a shot, or when a teammate spoke down to them, or when they lacked confidence in going for opportunities. I remember thinking, "I get it!" And I was still going through my own challenges; but as leaders, we don't have to be these complete, polished, fully finished products—we can be human works in progress. I was young and inexperienced, but I wanted to give these players what I had needed: positive energy, challenging them with love, and instilling a deep self-belief in each of them. Not viewing them as just their role on the team, but as the human under the helmet. You could even think of it as an experiment. As a leader, what happens if you genuinely care and support people?

> we can be human works in progress.

Before I took over the program, the team had never won a playoff game in school history. In that first year, we won the Los Angeles Championship. I was awarded US Lacrosse High School Coach of the Year in LA, the kids won awards, and we share a profound bond to this day. Believing in people, supporting them, and positively lifting them up is not some unessential, warm and fuzzy good feeling. I'm here to tell you it's how you achieve results. And it also feels great too.

Leadership that helps others will help you too.

Positivity isn't ignorance. In fact, it's the opposite. It's brave honesty, keen awareness, and in the moments when you identify that you are slipping into a negative spiral, it means stepping in as a leader to change it for yourself and the people who depend on you.

This isn't just a personal recommendation. The University of Michigan did a study on outlooks by looking at two sample groups. One with consistently negative outlooks, and one with consistently positive outlooks[7]. The group with positive outlooks had increased energy, better problem solving, and sharper motor skills. They had everything they needed to perform better. Not only is having a positive outlook a more fulfilling and enjoyable way to go through life, but it will lead to a heightened performance for yourself and the people you lead. Being positive is not a decorative garnish. It's how you cook a better meal.

I want to finish this lacrosse loop because it did come full circle, but I want to also point out that this book is not all jock examples. You don't have to get a helmet or even a giant foam finger. More than just sports, it's the human element of sports that is so powerful. I love athletics for a lot of reasons, one of which is how clear they make things. Life can sometimes get blurry. There can be a lot of gray area, but not in sports. It's all very clear. There are winners and losers. There are successful plays and missed opportunities, the points on the board, and the minutes left on the clock. There are starters, and then there are people who cry in a bathroom stall. I hope you never experience the humility and heartbreak of pretending to use the bathroom to muffle your tears.

After coaching to a championship and winning US Lacrosse Coach of the Year in Los Angeles, where I'd helped grow the sport, I was invited to grow the game internationally. I played and coached in over fifteen countries around the world, and I especially hit it off with the incredible members of the Argentinian Lacrosse Team. They were allotted three non-passport spots for their National Team that would then compete in the World Championship of Lacrosse—and they asked me to try out. An incredibly special honor!

This was a **big dream**. Growing up, my dad had taken me to the World Championships of Lacrosse in Baltimore, and I had a poster on my wall that I would look at through the years of being that bullied, insecure kid and dream of someday playing in it. All while I iced my chest bruises from Joey's bullying.

When I was accepted to try out, I felt that kid in me. I honored our promises, gave it everything I had, and I was selected to compete with Team Argentina in the World Championships of Lacrosse. It was *the* big dream, the "impossible" one the junior high me occasionally had fantasized about but decided was too big. It was *real*, and it was happening.

So, we shipped off to Tel Aviv to play in the World Championships. We suit up for our first game, sing the national anthems, get fired up in the huddle, and as I make my way onto the field for the opening whistle, something astonishing occurs that stops me in my tracks. I feel a surge of negativity—all the same feelings of fear and doubt that I had when I was nineteen years old getting benched on my college team and losing my first dream. It became very clear, because I kept fidgeting with my helmet, a nervous tick of mine when I was in college. But I'm not a teenager, I'm a grown man! I'm a terrific player, and I've even won awards coaching this sport. So, why am I still filled with doubt and fear of failing? Negativity, how are you still here?!

I realized at that moment that

> **we will never be immune to our fears. We will never be immune to our challenges, and we will never be immune to failing. But we can be immune to them stopping us.**

Right then, on the field of the World Championships of Lacrosse with the starting whistle about to blow—I needed *something*! But, what? Go watch *Rocky* real quick? Scream for a teammate to rush over and give me an emergency pep talk? No, just as before: there was nothing outside of me that could help me. What I needed was to lead myself as if I were leading someone who needed me. I instantly started listening to my positive energy voice and ignoring the fear voice. It was still there; I just wasn't paying attention to its rambles. I paired this with our promises: choosing to believe in myself, giving my best, taking big, bold actions—and I finished as a top goal scorer in the World Championships of Lacrosse. What meant the most was that this accomplishment felt like I was hugging my younger self. The kid defending his nips from Joey Lautner. The young man heartbroken after losing his dream. But this time, instead of crying in a bathroom stall hiding from my teammates, we were celebrating our success together—and Argentinians love to dance!

I hope this story can resonate with you. That you know you are capable of stepping up for yourself in the moments when you need it most. That if you do have fears right now, you can lower their volume. And if you have failed, know that it may just lead to one of your greatest successes.

LEAD YOURSELF

In those moments of adversity or uncertainty, whether spilling coffee, potentially losing a deal, or feeling your hands shake right before the presentation, how do you lead yourself at that moment? How are you speaking to yourself when you depend on you?

Could you speak to yourself as someone you are positively leading? You may even want to refer to yourself with an endearing nickname. I'll tell you mine. I call myself "Webs." I'll notice it in tough moments when I say to myself, "Alright, Webs, you need to focus up." "C'mon Webs, dig deep right now." Is that crazy? Maybe. I'm not embarrassed about this; I'm not embarrassed to be positive and to use tools to help me lead and perform better. By speaking to yourself, you're creating a separation between you and your mind. In that separation, you can actually step in to be a positive leader for yourself. So, grab yourself a nickname! Maybe you want to be a "Turbo" or a "Big M."

You could also give your negative voice a nickname. Maybe it's quite literally Negative Nancy! Or call it a Troll, or even think of it just as a scared little kid. See what clicks for you, but what's great about this is you are separating yourself from that voice. Because you are not that voice.

With a foundation of self-belief that has your best interest at heart, self-talk that supports you, and positive leadership for yourself and others—you're rock solid. And you're ready to take on the most important question you can ever ask.

Fail Proof Keys:

» Fear can misguide our good-hearted intentions and efforts.

» Leadership that helps others will help you too. As a leader, you can change someone's life at any moment.

» Positive self-talk increases performance, vitality, and results. Try leading yourself with a loving nickname or giving your negative voice a disempowering name.

The Most Important Question
You Can Ever Ask

— — — — — — — — — — — —

> *"The path from dreams to success does exist. May you have the vision to find it, the courage to get on it, and the perseverance to follow it."*
>
> —Kalpana Chawla, Astronaut, First Indian-born woman to go to space

One question changed my life.

It's the most important question you can ever ask yourself. I hinted at it earlier in this book. It's a question every person should ask themselves, often, in any situation. But the first time I asked, it wasn't until I was confused, searching, and scared for my future.

Your answer will be the foundation of your Fail Proof goals—the ones that mean the most to you, the goals that actually matter to your work, your relationships, and your life. To identify those goals, we need to know with brave honesty:

What do you want for your moments on Earth?

Now, this is an exciting question, but it's also tough to answer, right? First, fear can rob us of the excitement and make it imposing, pressure-filled, and overwhelming. What if you don't know the answer to this question? Or maybe you do know, but your fear is trying to convince you that it's impossible. It's not easy to tackle this question. And besides, who has the time? We rarely schedule a block on our calendar for "Life Questioning." We have obligations, deadlines, judgments from other people, and judgments from ourselves, and our phones just won't stop buzzing with updates and upgrades and notifications that need checking! It's A LOT. There's never a good time, and so we don't pick up our heads from the river current of our lives long enough to ask this question, answer it with brave honesty, and take positive action to make it our reality. We just keep going with the river. *Even though it's the most important question you can ever ask.*

So, let's drive home the truth about fear one more time, once and for all! Because if we don't, you will end up setting your Fail Proof goals based on your fears and not your true desires.

FEAR IS SCARED

You are not your fear. Fear is scared for you—which makes sense; that's pretty on-brand for fear. Fear's colleagues are scared too, the ones like negativity, doubt, anxiety, stress, pressure, and all of the internal forces that want to get in your way.

Here's the tragic thing. Those feelings are just trying to protect you. Fear is a misguided protector, like my dad with the math homework. Fear is screaming its opinion. *Opinion*, not *facts*. Fear is merely giving you its advice, and you don't have to take it. Imagine your voices as a potluck dinner, and fear brought expired, gray-looking mystery meat to the table. "Um, I'm going to pass on that one, fear." You can pass on fear's opinion when it comes to your goals too.

Your fear will always respond negatively when it comes to your big goals. "Don't go for it," "It's going to be hard," "It's unpromised," and "You may get hurt!" Now, fear isn't wrong. You may decide to go for these goals and encounter heartbreak, hurt, or humbling moments.

But if you listen to fear, ignore your heart's wishes, quit on your goals, and give up on yourself—is that without pain?

Is that without hurt, or heartbreak, or humbling moments? I've listened to fear and bailed on myself before—and, let me tell you, it's not painless. It is a deep, relentless, gnawing, and unforgiving pain that reminds you every single day that there is more for you, but you gave up on yourself. If you ask me, that hurts much more than failing ever could.

A Fail Proof life isn't without tough moments. But I promise you, it's a life without regrets. You will never feel that gut-wrenching pain ever again. Instead, you will experience waves of positive energy, the activation of your best qualities, and a surge that builds more and more momentum toward your highest goals, because you are honoring what you truly want for yourself and the people who need you.

ZOOM OUT TO ZOOM IN

Claiming these Fail Proof goals is so impactful because they'll serve as your North Star.

> **According to researchers out of Cornell University, we make 35,000 decisions a day.[8] Your Fail Proof goals will guide these decisions—consciously and unconsciously.**

They will guide your actions, your behavior, and where you give your time, energy, and focus. That's why it's so essential to determine what you want thoughtfully and with brave honesty.

To help you do that, I want to introduce a bit of perspective. Let's zoom out before we zoom in. And I mean zoom all the way out.

Regardless of what you, me, or anyone else believes about life. These are facts:

- Earth is a planet. It is a planet in infinite space.
- You are a living creature on this planet in infinite space.
- You have a limited amount of heartbeats, breaths, and moments you get to live on this planet in infinite space.

Maybe there's an afterlife; maybe there's not. Maybe there's reincarnation; maybe there's not. But you—right now—here—living this life is a one-of-one deal. And it's a pretty great deal.

First off, Earth is a terrific spot. Hands down, my favorite planet. The second-best planet for life is Mars, but only because Mars *might* have bacteria in a puddle. As far as being a living creature goes, we got dealt a sweet hand just by being born here.

We all fall victim to the pressures of expectations, bills, deadlines, social media, bank accounts, criticisms, and life crises. But please don't ever let that rob you of the simple truth that this is a magically wonderful life we get to live. So, let's talk about how we can make your life magically wonderful for you.

What do you want for your moments on Earth?

To help, let's explore (which means without judgment) these vital and impactful questions:

What does success look like to you?

What do you want to do?

Who do you want to become?

What do you want to lead?

I've asked these questions often. Sometimes these questions were scarier than others. And sometimes the answers themselves were quite scary. Not scary like a horror film where they go back in the house to get that snarky friend, Andy, even though we know the killer is waiting, "Just leave Andy! He had it coming!" I mean real fear. Deep fear where you're terrified for your future.

I felt that fear on a gorgeous Friday afternoon in Los Angeles sitting on the 405 freeway in bumper to bumper traffic while being honked at by angry Prius drivers. I had just left the offices of NBC Universal—and I was heartbroken. But I was also *deeply excited*. Before I can tell you about that moment, I need to tell you about the first time I ever asked our most important questions.

The first time was when I was a senior in college, playing Division I lacrosse, and on my way to a career in finance, which is certainly a great path. But it wasn't great *for me*. I realized this my senior fall; and with every finance course, internship, and job interview, the more I was certain it wasn't right for me. And yet, I still kept heading toward it because that's where the river current of life had brought me. I didn't think it was possible to change it, or even really know how to change it, and I kind of thought it might be too late to change it anyways. So I just kept going with it, even though I knew it wasn't right for me. Have you ever done something like that? Where you keep going with the river current even though part of you *knows* it isn't right.

One night, a few of my close friends and I decided to make a campfire—which we'd never done before. I went to school in Philadelphia; there were no woods. And by "campfire," I mean we doused old magazines in lighter fluid and lit them into a glossy blaze. Lovely ambiance. Slightly woozy off magazine fumes, we sat around and talked about life. What we each thought about life, what we wanted for ourselves, and what being successful might mean to each of us. The exact questions you and I are exploring right now. Believe it or not, even with loving family, friends, and people in my life, this was the first time I'd ever truly picked up my head from the river current to asked these questions.

That night, I just allowed myself to answer with brave honesty. I quieted my negative, fearful mind, and allowed the real me to speak.

The next morning, I read what I wrote, which was difficult, because my handwriting looks like a rooster tried cursive. But it was so clear to me that the goals I'd been chasing weren't ones I really wanted. I realized, "Wait, I don't want this for my life. And if I don't want this for my life, then why am I giving my life to making it happen?"

That morning, I stopped. I stopped giving my heartbeats to a path that wasn't right for me, and I started down a new path that was.

The only things I knew for sure were that I was petrified for my future, and so deeply excited for it.

What I wrote down that night was that I wanted to: positively help people and be a performer. Two pretty unlinked goals, but the heart wants what it wants!

So, I did it, and I did it with big, bold action. I left my secure job path, left all my friends, family, home, and came out to Hollywood to be a performer. Is that a cliché? Hard to say. But a few years later, after my chapter coaching lacrosse, I was hired by NBC to host a series for *American Ninja Warrior*. I was hired to be a performer, and it's for a series that positively helps millions. Dream job alert!

I'll never forget walking onto the *American Ninja Warrior* set for the first time. It's massive. They say things from TV are smaller in person. Not here! The *ANW* set is towering, magnificent, imposing, and exhilarating. There are tons of people buzzing around setting up the course, lights, and cameras; athletes swinging on obstacles; and the city's locals flocking out to see the spectacle. It's genuinely electric. Here I was, hitting one of my dream goals: performing for NBC for a sports competition (we know I love sports!) and it powerfully motivates and encourages people. I don't know if you believe in a higher power, but I thank something bigger than myself for giving me that opportunity. And also, of course, NBC Universal.

I loved this job, and I was great at it. Good enough, in fact, to win an award with NBC! I grew up watching NBC hits like *Seinfeld* ("Newman!") and *FRIENDS* ("we were on a break!") and now I've won an award hosting a series for NBC that inspires millions! Incredible. Surreal. Heart-bursting amazingness, and then suddenly—it ended. We wrapped. Finished. Over. Done! Just like that. I'll never forget when one of the Executive Producers told me "Alex, congrats! Now as you know, the series is not coming back." But I did *not* know it wasn't coming back. And that's when I remember so vividly driving back from NBC on that Friday afternoon when it ended. In my stomach, I had that all too familiar feeling. Queasy. Scared. But most of all, heartbroken. I loved this job so much, I loved the community so much, and now it was gone. So, sitting there in traffic while Prius drivers continued to honk, I asked myself yet again:

What do you want for your moments on earth?

What does success look like to you?

What do you want to do?

Who do you want to become?

What do you want to lead?

And that's when the *excitement* came in. Because even though I felt heartbreak and fear for my future, once I started to explore these questions with brave honesty, that's when I began to actually feel excited for what might come next. Answering these questions and honoring our Fail Proof Promises is what led me to my next dream of becoming an international keynote speaker, combining performing with positively helping people all around the world. It's also what led me to come back to *America Ninja Warrior*, but this time as a competitor. A dream I could have never even imagined, and I'm so deeply thankful for it.

Now, sometimes we ask these questions, and the answers involve enormous changes to our lives where we uproot and go full pioneer mode, seeking out our destiny. But that's not always the case. And good thing it's not; that sounds exhausting.

Sometimes, we just take a look at our work, or our relationships, or how we're leading our lives, and we simply say, **"I'd like for this to be better,"** or maybe, **"I feel like there's more for me here."**

Take a moment and allow yourself that fearless exploration to brainstorm answers. There is no right or wrong, and there is no too big or too small. This is an idea board right now. Lay it all out there and keep adding as things pop in your head. We'll get to focusing in on your Fail Proof goals next, but right now, we need to get all the ideas out of your head and into this world. Have some fun with this!

What do you want for your moments on Earth?

*And remember to run these questions through your different areas: your work, your relationships, and your life.

What does success look like to you?

- *"Reaching our highest quarter yet."*
- *"Deeply connected to my partner."*
- *"Cooperation, ease, and trust between myself and my colleagues."*

What do you want to do?

- *"Run a half marathon."*
- *"Get ten more clients."*
- *"Buy a house."*

Who do you want to become?

- *"The best version of myself."*
- *"A leader at my work."*
- *"An amazing friend and family member."*

What do you want to lead?

- *"My department's new project."*
- *"A loving, supportive family."*
- *"I want to positively lead myself."*

Fear is going to scream in your ear: "What if it doesn't work out?!" But that fear is not you. That fear is just scared for you, and it doesn't know the transformation taking place within you. You are becoming unstoppable. Fear may be strong. But you are stronger.

Fail Proof Keys:

» What do you want for your moments on Earth? Explore with brave honesty.

» Take a look at your work, your relationships, and your life. Allow yourself to write any and all ideas that come to mind!

» Ignore the voice of fear right now. Fear may be strong, but you are stronger.

THE FAIL PROOF SYSTEM: BECOMING UNSTOPPABLE

8

Step 1. Claim Your Fail Proof Goals

"If you set your goals ridiculously high and it's a failure, you will fail above everyone else's success."
—James Cameron, Academy Award-Winning Filmmaker

You can do, become, and lead anything you want with this system. So: What do you want to do? Who do you want to become? What do you want to lead?

You've been exploring these questions with brave honesty, and now we're getting ready to claim our Fail Proof goals. Goals that you truly want for your work, your relationships, and your life. Ambitious, high-achieving, dream-caliber goals. It's okay if they seem daunting or uncomfortable, or make part of you even question, "How the heck is that going to happen for me?!" That's great, that's what they should be, because remember, you will be using the Fail Proof System to become unstoppable in making these happen. So, set these Fail Proof goals high!

Now one more note as you hone in on your Fail Proof goals. Honor what is important to *you*, because caring is such a unique force. We as people have this incredible ability to care or not care about so many different things. For example, there is a Fondue Club in Nova Scotia, aptly called *Club Fondue*. Every week, these fine folks get together to talk about the best practices of melting cheese and ideal breads for dipping. Now, I'm going to bet my butt that you don't care about *Club Fondue*. Maybe I'm wrong! (But, I'm not wrong.) And how great is that? There are so many wonderful things in this world to care about—or not care about.

Not everything you care about needs to be important to everyone else, including your friends, or colleagues, or loved ones, or me, or random people off the internet. There is no right or wrong answer, so long as it is your answer. You have complete autonomy over what you care about, just like our cheesy friends up north.

> **The truth is that nothing matters in this world—*nothing*— except what you decide matters. When you decide that something matters, then it means everything. And what matters to you may be unique to you.**

Your Fail Proof goals don't need to be something extreme either, like climbing Mount Kilimanjaro with a documentary crew that somehow raises money for three-legged puppies to also climb Mount Kilimanjaro. Fail Proof goals can be anything! That's the fun of them. Maybe it's looking at your career and thinking, "I'd love to lead this project." Or perhaps it's looking at your relationships and thinking, "I want to let this person see this side of me," or, looking yourself in the mirror and admitting, "I want to feel better about myself."

So take a look at your work, your relationships, your personal life, and ask yourself: **what matters to me here, and what would I like to be better?**

Why these goals mean something to us is incredibly powerful as well. As I write this to you, I'm training to compete again on *American Ninja Warrior.* Swinging from enormous obstacles might mean nothing to some people, but it means so much to me for so many reasons. One reason is that it authentically causes me to stand for what I believe in, and what I am encouraging you to do—positively lead yourself beyond failures to reach your highest goals! If I talk the talk as an international keynote speaker, this is my chance to walk the walk. Or more accurately, crazy leap the crazy leap. It means something to my relationships. I've met some of my best friends in the world through this sport. And it means something to me living my life. It makes me feel like anything is possible. If I can be more fearless now than I've ever been before, and do things that I never thought I could do—then what else may be possible?

Last night, I drove an hour to the one specific Ninja Gym in our city, trained for four hours getting flung off obstacles until late at night, drove an hour back, couldn't fall asleep because I'm all revved up, and now write these pages to you while I have healing balm on my hands because they are so freaking sore, and my keyboard is now sticky.

Here's the beautiful thing. Because this goal matters so much to me, I feel truly grateful for all the experiences. I'm so incredibly excited and thankful for the late hours, long workouts, all the challenges, setbacks, pressures, and, yes, failures. In any of those moments, if we take a step back and remember how much these goals mean to us, then it will re-focus away from the negative voice and back to the positive energy of fulfillment, gratitude, and success.

Now here is what's cool. As we said, nothing exists in a vacuum, just like how the negative voice is a toxic oil spill that can ripple into all areas of your life. The same is the case in the positive direction. By focusing on goals that actually matter, you will activate your best qualities. You genuinely want these goals to happen, so that will trigger more focus, energy, effort, creativity, and resourcefulness within you. That best version of you that has more focus, energy, effort, creativity, and resourcefulness is going to be the same you that shows up at work, shows up in your relationships, and shows up for yourself. These Fail Proof goals will ignite the best of yourself, and you will see benefits in all areas of your life.

> *These Fail Proof goals will ignite the best of yourself, and you will see benefits in all areas of your life.*

EVERYTHING IS POSSIBLE WHEN YOU'RE UNSTOPPABLE

One final key before you claim your Fail Proof goals. Sometimes, I think we can develop a false belief that we are not qualified to do something. We don't have the credentials, or the skillset, or maybe our life situation just doesn't present us with the chance to do what we want to do. To that I say: **everything is possible when you're unstoppable.**

Your fear is the voice that is telling you that you cannot do something. It's grasping at some loose facts in the world to piece together its ragtag case of why you shouldn't go for your goals. For instance, it may say "You're not an expert! Only experts can do that." Well, good thing there are no such things as experts in this world. I'm going to say that again. *I believe that there are no such things as experts.* I don't care where someone went to school, what degrees they have on their wall, or what fancy title it says on LinkedIn (you can just make those up, FYI).

> **There are no experts in this world; there are only people who care about what they do, show up, and do their best every moment. And then there are people who don't.**

Now what's exciting is that means if you do care about what you do, show up, and do your best, then there are no limits to what you can do, become, and lead. Just because you don't have that job title yet, or you've never done it before, or you don't have the degree on the wall, does not mean you can't do it. There were plenty of degrees on the wall of the doctor who missed my mom's cancer. Lots of accolades with the next doctor who said she wouldn't make it a year. With anything in life, there are good ones and bad ones of everything. Great pizza shops and cruddy ones. People who give you a great haircut, and people who make you look like they used safety scissors. Just because someone has a sign out front or a degree on the wall, or they call themselves a prestigious title, doesn't mean they are terrific at it. And it also means that you can be excellent at it even if you don't have the sign or degree or even call yourself that thing just yet. There's an incredible opportunity in that for you. It's liberating! Yes, you'll of course need to keep growing, learning, improving, and embracing possibilities ("failing")—and that's where this Fail Proof System comes in for you. All you need to know now is that you are fully capable of leveling up in your work, fully able to better your relationships, and fully qualified to elevate your life.

Right now, you only need to believe that these goals may be possible for you. And only you need to believe it, because people don't see it until they see it. That needs to be said again. *People don't see it until they see it.* What I mean by that is not everyone is going to see your raw potential or amazing ideas or hidden abilities or the sheer will within you to become what you'd like to be in this world—but when you show it, they'll excitedly join in your vision and probably act like they've seen it the whole time. Take it from Stan Lee, one of the creative leaders of Marvel Comics, which is worth $4 billion. Stan Lee had an idea for a superhero that he really believed had potential. The character was unique in that he behaved like, well, not everyone's favorite creature: a spider. When he brought it into this publisher's office, he was ridiculed and had his idea thrown out. His publisher lashed, "People hate spiders! This is terrible!" But Stan Lee felt in his heart that there was something compelling about this web-spewing character he had created, and so he gave it a true best shot. And, instead of that idea being in a folder labeled, "Ideas I love but didn't give a shot," it's now called *Spider-Man*, and has grossed over $6.3 billion in movie ticket sales alone. And guess who was the first one to celebrate *Spider-Man*'s initial success? Yup, the publisher who shamed the idea out of the room.

> **The point is this: not everyone needs to believe in your idea, or your potential, or *you*. You just need to believe in you and act upon it.**

When people do start to see it, it can be incredibly encouraging. In my life, I'll never forget how amazing it felt to have a top speaker call me "the real deal" after my first big keynote. Or when American Ninja Warriors showed me respect me as a competitor. All of that felt very validating, but let's not fall into the trap of attaching our self-worth to other people's beliefs. Remember, we have no control over those, and they can change at any instant for any reason. Any reason! Instead, let's keep focused on cultivating true, consistent, reliable self-belief in yourself. That is your foundation.

So right now, think of your Fail Proof goals and understand that even if no one sees it just yet, and even if you don't fully believe it yourself just yet—you still are capable of doing it, becoming it, and leading it. That is the power of claiming these goals for yourself and the people who need you.

YOUR FAIL PROOF GOALS

Claim these goals! Claim what you really want for yourself and the people in your life. Set these Fail Proof goals high. In the words of my mom, "if you're going to do it, do it." Full transparency, she told me this when she saw me eat only half a cookie, but I think the lesson applies to everything. If you're going to do it, do it. If you're going to commit your heartbeats to these goals—make them big.

Look at your brainstormed list and then write down these Fail Proof goals. Declare them, and start to feel it already. Go about your day as the person who's already making these goals happen—because you are already making these goals happen right now.

MY FAIL PROOF GOALS:

In my work:

In my relationships:

In my life:

How did it feel writing those down? Exciting? Unrealistic? Maybe a combo platter? Good. Anything worth anything feels that way. The journey has now begun. Your coordinates are set, keep your eyes to this North Star and grab some granola, because we're heading to the mountain peak!

Fail Proof Keys:

» Fail Proof goals will ignite the best of yourself, and you will see benefits in all areas of your life.

» Your Fail Proof goals only need to matter to you. No one else needs to see it or believe in it yet.

» Claim these goals. Take ownership and pride in declaring this for yourself!

Step 2. Make It Real: Build Your Momentum

"It is so much easier not to do things than to do them, that you would do anything is totally remarkable. Percentage-wise, it is 100% easier not to do things than to do them."

—John Mulaney, Comedian

Going after goals is hard! But by claiming your Fail Proof goals, you've already taken the first step toward making them a reality. Now, it's time to make it *real*. How we're going to do that is by identifying what you can do right now to bring it out of "idea-land" and put it into the real world—your real life.

So, first, let's see if we can clear some obstacles out of the way. Let me ask you this: could your goal be a reality right now? If yes, well, job well done! If no, why? What is standing in the way of your goal being a reality? Is it time? Is it a skillset? It is just not knowing how and where to take that first step?

Is it being fearful of taking that step because of what it could mean or what people might do, say, or think? How specific can you identify the key challenge that is standing in the between you and your goal being a reality?

Try this exercise. List out the reasons why your goal isn't happening right now. Go ahead, dump 'em all!

…(keep going)…

Now, let's make sure we're wearing our lenses of brave honesty and we clean off that gunky build-up of fear. Many leaders and high-achievers hit a wall because they are unable to honor our first promise of brave honesty with this step. Whether consciously or not, their fears simply won't allow them to be bravely honest *and* specific on what needs to change.

Ambiguity is where goals die. Don't fall into that trap. Honor our promises together and revisit that list. How specific can you get on the real challenges (outside of you or inside of you) that are standing in the way of your goal becoming a reality?

> Ambiguity is where goals die. Don't fall into that trap.

For instance, let's say you've identified:

"I want to pitch a new project idea to my boss, but it's not really my job title, and my colleagues may take offense. Specifically, Rachel."

"I need to tell a family member that they're doing something that really upsets me and has upset me for a long time, but I'm scared it might turn into a fight and just make things worse."

"I'd love to play the piano; I've always wanted to do it. But I don't have time to learn the piano, and I don't own a piano or really want to spend the money to get a piano, and now I'm starting to hate the word piano."

These are bravely honest statements, and because they're bravely honest, they're clear and we can work with them. We can explore these statements to identify the real, key challenge. For instance, in the example of pitching the new project idea, the key challenge is not just pitching the idea but the way in which your colleagues may react; even more so, it is the way that Rachel may react. Similarly, for the conversation with the loved one, it is not the conversation, it is the fear that the conversation may turn into a fight. With the piano, all of these may or may not be accurate reasons, but the brave honesty comes in really getting clear on which of these is actually the stopping point. Is it the time, is it the logistics of not owning a piano, or is the financial commitment of purchasing one? Time, logistics, and finances are all challenges that can be handled, if you know which one you need to handle. If we get clear on the *real* stopping point—the key challenge—then we can begin to navigate past it.

Look at your Fail Proof goals and look at why they're not a reality right now. What is the main stopping point in the way? There might be a few that come to mind, but poke at them with brave honesty, because when you do hit the challenge that is really standing in the way, you're going to know it. Your body, gut, and mind are going to instinctively tell you, "Yeah that's the one, that's why." Really listen, because the negative voice of fear may be trying to run interference to your clarity. That voice of your fears, uncertainties, pressures, stress, anxiety, nerves, and doubts is eagerly waiting to chow down, like a hungry dog ready for you to place its bowl on the ground. Look at your fears, uncertainties, pressures, stress, anxiety, nerves, and doubts, and say, "Sit." In fact, tell them to sit until they quiet down and then place their bowl outside, because we have work to do in here. You may still hear a bark here and there, but focus your attention on your true voice of positive energy and self-belief. Then: identify the key challenge standing in the way of your Fail Proof goals.

When you do, write it down. Standing in my way is

"my uncertainty around what Rachel and my colleagues may think."

"my fear of what my loved one may do when I confront them."

"that I don't have time to learn the piano."

Now, what can you do to remove this stop sign?

Your goal's full realization cannot be accomplished today, so don't even waste a second sweating over that. All that is going to do is make it feel daunting and impossible. Instead, get excited about this action you can take today.

For instance:

Could you message a close colleague, maybe even Rachel, and let them know of your desire to pitch this idea while asking them for some support or feedback? Including them rather than excluding them.

For the tough conversation with someone you love, could you look at why conversations in the past have escalated to fights? For this conversation, is there a way to diffuse it?

Perhaps predicting what incites them, or even coming into the conversation with a greater sense of empathy or understanding for why they may be doing what they're doing?

For that good ol' piano, if time is really the key challenge, where can you find this time? You know your life's moments better than anybody else, so with brave honesty, are there ten minutes that you can find in your day to learn something you've always wanted in your life? Maybe it's accountability. Sign up for a piano teacher today, and while you fill out the sign-up form, play your favorite pianist's concerto as you feel yourself fill up with excitement. *Bravissimo!*

In the next chapter, we will take big, bold actions—because you are capable of them, and that is what really shifts your life—but right now, let's spark the momentum. Any forward step is a huge step right now. You have just brought this goal out of "idea-land" and into the real world. Science even shows that any positive momentum massively increases our chances for success[9]. Tap into it right now. Switch the script from this imposing, daunting challenge that left you powerless to just a temporary stop sign that slowed you down, but now you're about to hit the gas and go forward, beginning right now.

If we were to visualize our hike to the mountain peak of your goals, then this step right now is lacing up your hiking boots and getting on the mountain. You may have a map of the route to the top, or maybe you don't, and that's okay.

> **You don't need to know the whole plan right now; you only need to know this step.**

It's very possible, in fact, that the following action can only be revealed by taking this step right now. Like a trail that's hidden behind trees and brush. Even if we had a map, the next best step might not be on it. You only need to choose to believe in yourself in this moment, take this action to make your goal real, and believe that you will be capable of taking the next step, and the next step as they unfold before you.

IT IS THAT SIMPLE

You do know what you need to do. More so, you know why you're not doing it. If you turn down the volume on the negative voice and allow yourself to be bravely honest, then you know what is standing in the way of your goals, and you also know the first action toward making them happen. This small yet meaningful action will begin the powerful process of forward momentum. I'm asking you to be bravely honest, choose to believe in yourself, and give your best. It is that simple.

"That's the biggest lie I was ever told: 'It's not that simple,'" said Vinny Paz, the world champion boxer who recovered from a spinal injury. "It's how they get you to give up." He goes on to elaborate that the truth is that it is that simple. "That if you just do the thing that they tell you that you can't, then it's done. And you realize it is that simple…. And it always was." I love his perspective. By convincing ourselves our goals are complicated, complex, and huge, then it justifies us quitting. It causes us to lose sight of the fact that accomplishing any goal is as simple as taking meaningful action right now. Then doing it again, and again, and again, until you pick up your head and your goals are your reality.

It is this simple.

But we pile on these layers of opinions from other people, judgments from ourselves, our fears, expectations, and that sneaky layer of playing it safe even though we will regret it. We pile on so many layers that we can't even see the simple truth anymore.

> So, let me be your loving reminder here. If you look for things to blame, you will find them. But if you look for the positive actions, you will find them too, and they'll feel a whole lot better than the blame game.

My dad is not a poetic man, but one day he said to me, "Zander" (he calls me Zander—well, technically it sounds like "Zanda" because he's from Long Island, and it's obligatory that you have that accent). "Zanda," he said, "things lead to things."

I paused and replied, "Dad, that might be the truest thing I've ever heard." Things lead to things. You don't need to know all of the things right now. You don't. You just need to know that if you take this step, then the next one will show itself. Let me rephrase that. *You just need to believe in yourself that if you take this step, and give your best to it, then it will lead to a next step, where you will then give your best.* You are building the staircase as you go, and you will do it.

> You are building the staircase as you go, and you will do it.

After my dream job of being an award-winning host for *American Ninja Warrior* ended, I was driving back from that NBC meeting heartbroken, yet again, while inhaling LA traffic fumes. That moment where I asked myself the most important question we can ever ask, "What do I want for my moments on Earth?" my answer came back, "I want to be a speaker. A speaker who uses entertainment and positive energy to help people." I had zero idea how that would happen, but the first step was to put it into the world. I reached out to someone who was loosely affiliated with the world of TED Talks. They sent me a generic application form to apply. So, I did. That was the only step I could see. And in the next year, I was a speaker and gave five TEDx Talks.

You may hear, "you don't need to see the whole staircase, you just need to take the first step." I agree, but also remember: You are building your staircase. You have the wood, the nails, and your hammer. Choose to believe in yourself, give your best, and *build* your momentum—cause we're about to build big!

Fail Proof Keys:

» With brave honesty, what is the key challenge standing in the way of your goal being a reality?

» Seize this first step. You don't need to see every step after that. You are building the staircase as you go, and you will do it.

» What is the first step to make your Fail Proof goal *real*?

Step 3. Dive In Or Belly Flop: Just Get In The Water!

- - - - - - - - - - - - - -

"And that's what separates sometimes the people who do things from those who just dream about them. You gotta act. You gotta be willing to fail. You gotta be willing to crash and burn...if you're afraid you'll fail, you won't get very far."
—Steve Jobs, Founder of Pixar and Apple

The most critical thing you can ever do is to start. You just identified your first step, and with that, you've started. Out of a complete standstill, a goal collecting dust on a shelf, or fear convincing you that it was impossible, now you've brought it into the real-world, you've made it a possibility, AND you've created positive momentum. You are the creator of your story! How about that?! Now, it's time go big and bold.

It's like when you were growing up during a hot summer day, and you wanted to find a pool you could swim in. So, you ask around, you put your feelers out, and you find that one kid,

Jamie, has got a pool. You're not even good friends with Jamie, but you put on your sweet talk, chum it up, maybe even bring some ice pops, and next thing you know, you're standing at the edge of a shimmering swimming pool.

Now let me ask you something: It's ninety degrees, you've hustled all day to get to this pool's edge, and you are finally looking out over the glistening water. Do you hesitantly dip your toe in—or do you cannonball in with an epic splash?!

When it comes to your goals, actions are no different. When it comes to the waters of what you want to do, do not dip your toe.

> **Leap. Dive in the deep-end, even if it's a glorious belly flop. Ugly, imperfect, maybe even a little raw and stinging. It doesn't matter. All that matters is that you took big, bold action, and now you're in the water.**

And I'll tell you why.

Sometimes a goal seems so daunting that even when we work up the nerve to give it a shot, we can fall into the trap of only giving it a hesitant attempt because we're scared it won't go well. When you give it this hesitant attempt, it not only goes poorly because you're restraining your effort and all initial attempts aren't perfect anyways—but it also feels overwhelming and impossible because there's still this ambiguity around your goal separating you from the center of the action.

Here's the game-changing truth. Say you didn't give this a light, hesitant, non-committal attempt, but you gave it everything you have, and you dove into the deepest end, the heart of the action. You didn't hold back because of fear that it wouldn't go well or people might judge you, and you even did it with people who are way more qualified, experienced, and flat out better at this than you. BIG and BOLD! What will happen is that it will remove all of this ambiguity, mystery, and doubt. You very well may perform horribly, but you're performing horribly while *being in the heart of it*! You have torn down all these barriers between you and what you want for yourself. You've eliminated the variables of uncertainty, and now you have an honest baseline from which you can improve. That baseline very well may be: "Wow, I am terrible at this!" (I've been there.) But that is exactly how you would have felt with that hesitant, safe-distanced attempt. It's a constant. So instead of feeling that way and also feeling uncertain of how you might go forward, now you are a part of it, it's happening, and you know what you can do to get better. There are so many benefits to what I call the "Deep End Effect."

THE DEEP END EFFECT

My loving challenge to you is for you to identify a big, bold action where you can dive into the deep end of your goal. Call the office of the CEO and ask for a five minute conversation. Take your loved ones away for an off-the-grid trip. Show up to the Jiu Jitsu class and jump in. Overwhelming? Yup! But only for a little while. Instead of standing by and allowing our false fears to grow more powerful, you are becoming more powerful. Think of all the qualities within you that will be activated by doing these big, bold actions. You are going to have to be confident, have presence of mind, commit to yourself, follow through on it, and think sharply too. And when you do, that version of you is also going to perform better! The answer is big, bold action.

This will expedite your process and help you by giving factual evidence to beat your negative voice of fear. Fears thrive in uncertainty and inaction, but with these big, bold actions, fear will have less ground to stand on, no matter what the result. When fear starts voicing its opinions of doubt, trying to convince you to stop, they'll seem illogical, because you can point to your evidence and say, "Hold on, fear. Yeah, that first attempt wasn't great, but now I know where I need to improve and I'm doing it. So, stop judging every brick that I put down, and let me build this house!" Fear is very impatient and horrible at building.

There was a very unique year of my life that brought this truth to an *extreme*.

When I first made the decision to become elite at *American Ninja Warrior*, I had to begin training with elite American Ninja Warriors. This was when the Fail Proof System became so crystal clear to me, because, well, I was failing at such a high frequency. I was failing *so much*, over and over again—and it was getting to me. It showed up in how I reacted to falling short, how I'd interact with the competitors, and even how I'd feel about myself at the end of the night. I wasn't just way out of my league; I was out of my world!

First off, I'd pull up to these warehouses on the outskirts of cities where people constructed what looks like a massive, medieval jungle gym. Ropes and chains and dangling balls hanging in the air from steel rafters. It's confusing, exciting, and scary all at the same time. Not to mention very, very difficult. My colleagues here are incredibly gifted athletes who are also incredible human beings and just so happen to be the coolest kids in town.

> They're doing backflips off Wranglers (literally), and I look like the new kid who got lost on his way to buy khakis at the Gap.

It was incredibly overwhelming. People are swinging off bars, bouncing off walls, and flipping every which way. I wouldn't even know where to stand. "Am I in your way? Oh, no, you'll just flip over me? Cool."

As a result of simply jumping in with these top athletes, I would fail over and over again. I failed impressively hard. It would get to the point where I was failing nineteen and twenty times an hour. If I stewed over each one, the gym would close, and I'd still be there wallowing in the parking lot. That's actually how the Fail Proof System was born: I needed to expedite the failing process, because there just wasn't enough time for all my fails. That realization was a beautiful gift; thanks to my seemingly endless failings, I was able to distill the fail process down to a quick-fire sequence that happens every single time. We are beginning this sequence right now with these big, bold actions in the deep end, and I will continue to give you each of the steps as we progress in the Fail Proof System.

As I got clarity on this system, I was getting better. I could see my progress. Even though I was the newb, I was still working alongside the best. Taking cues from what they do, picking up pointers, and being challenged to train at their level. More than anything, I realized that even though my negative voice convinced me that these competitors thought I was a no-good imposter, they actually didn't think that at all. Instead, they recognized that I shared their love and commitment, and so they were incredibly generous with their time, energy, and coaching to make me better. This is one of the virtues of diving in the deep end.

I want to add one more fail layer to this. You see, during this time of diving into the deepest end of training with American Ninja Warriors was also when I was the host for NBC (and still dealing with my own insecurities and fear of failing); and on top of that, I was stepping into another dream of mine: stand-up comedy. Which most people agree is one of the easiest things to do…

During those years of bullying, when I was an insecure teen being made fun of and eating lunch alone in the math room, comedy was my savior. I would geek out listening to stand-up comedy, and I'd even crack little jokes in classes to entertain people (read: to get people to like me). I always wanted to do stand-up, but I was scared. It's so hard! You're in front of a room of strangers; who knows what they're thinking about you; and you need their approval in the form of a very vocal response. When you succeed in stand-up, there is an obvious result: laughs. And when you are failing, or bombing, well—no laughs. Crickets. One minute feels like an eternity. Because I was scared of failing at it, I'd only give it a hesitant, non-committal attempt from a safe distance, and guess what happened? Nothing. Stand-up comedy didn't become a part of my life. It was just a dream goal that instead of building momentum was building regret inside of me.

So, I had a bravely honest moment with myself. I asked our most important question, and I decided I needed to dive into the deep end with an epic belly flop—so I did. I would go to stand-up comedy shows every night, not knowing a single person, and awkwardly try to meet comedians. I would desperately try to start conversations, "So ice is just frozen water; crazy, right?" But when I refocused to sincerity, that's when things changed. When I actually approached comedians, told them I admired their work, that I had a dream of becoming a stand-up comedian, that's when the Deep End Effect happened. They saw I shared their love and commitment, and so they were generous with their time, energy, and coaching to make me better. I'm not going to say that everyone in the world will give you this response, but I am going to say that you will be pleasantly surprised by the amount of people who do. But it begins with you belly flopping in.

After a few weeks, one comic even offered to produce a weekly show with me. We did it Friday nights above a Mexican restaurant. Half our pre-show was setting up chairs, and the other half was begging restaurant patrons to take their guacamole upstairs to hear us tell jokes. I remember my first time doing that stand-up show, specifically how I didn't make a single person laugh for fifteen minutes. One minute feels like an eternity. So, fifteen minutes feels like you're being tarred and feathered in the underworld. I was sweating so much and starting to blackout from the overall horribleness of the experience, but I could just barely make out when a sweet lady in the front row asked me, "Are you okay?"

Now, just to be clear: failing at stand-up comedy and failing at *American Ninja Warrior* were happening simultaneously. I was failing horribly at *American Ninja Warrior* by day, climbing on gigantic, wobbling, spinning obstacles and getting flung to the ground. Then, I was failing horribly at stand-up by night, telling not-funny jokes to a room of strangers while they didn't laugh, and I sweat through every shirt I own. I did this for a year. I'm not exaggerating.

I failed by day and failed by night for one year straight, and I'm so thankful for it.

It forced me to get over it. You see, before that time, I'd get so worked up and caught in my own emotions or judgments or discouragements from failing, but now, I was failing too often for any of that. I couldn't beat myself up after every failure. There just wasn't enough time!

Lessons, tools, and strategies that got me through my year of failing turned me into an *American Ninja Warrior* competitor and *succeeding* on the course. It allowed me to do stand-up comedy around the world, but instead of crickets, I heard laughs in New York City, London, Toronto, Vienna, and Budapest. It even allowed me to co-found a business running the largest live comedy series in America. It gave me the confidence and foundation to become a professional speaker, positively impacting over 3.5 million people worldwide to achieve their highest goals.

And here's a final cool, and illuminating, factoid. Want to know one of the most common pieces of advice said by both stand-up comedians and elite American Ninja Warriors? *Commit.* In comedy, you commit to the bit. If you don't, the audience feels it and you don't get laughs. In *American Ninja Warrior,* you commit to the dynamic leaps and grabs you need to make. If you don't, not only will you miss—but you will hurt yourself. I could go on and on with examples of the power of fully committing to you and the actions that will bring you to your goal—but the choice will always be yours.

No matter how discouraging, daunting, heartbreaking, or humiliating any of your failures may have been up to this point, I assure you that you will blow past them with this system and committing to yourself. And it all starts with diving in the deep end. Remember, whether you hesitantly dip your toe or cannon ball in the deepest end, you're going to get wet either way, so you might as well make a splash.

Fail Proof Keys:
- » How can you jump in the deep end of your goals?
- » Remember, even if it's a belly flop, you'll still:
  - o tear down the mystery and receive an honest baseline of where you are at.
  - o uncover real knowledge and experience for how you can improve.
  - o connect with people who will foster your growth.
- » Make a splash! And it will supercharge your momentum.

Step 4. Respond, Don't React: Managing Your Emotions

"Failure happens all the time. It happens every day in practice. What makes you better is how you react to it."
—Mia Hamm, 2x Olympic Gold Medalist and World Cup Champion

Have you ever been in a good mood, and then for some reason, it tanks—but you can't even really remember what shifted it or pinpoint why you're now in a funk? Maybe it was the pressure of a deadline. Maybe it was receiving an email from a colleague saying a project is going to need yet more work. Maybe it was seeing a competitor being farther along than you. Maybe it was just noticing a bill on your desk. "Why does my internet charge me for a landline phone? A _landline_ phone!"

We're emotional beings, and a lot of those emotions can be unpredictable. You could even say that their unpredictability is predictable. When emotions really flare up is when we hit resistance, disappointment, or a setback...you know, FAIL. I said that failing is a process of growing, improving, and embracing possibilities—and it's an *emotional* process.

> **The greatest definer of your life is what you do in the moments of adversity.**

So many people allow those moments to be dictated by negative emotions, lingering setbacks, lack of self-belief, indulging criticisms from external or internal voices, and it results in backing away from the goal.

Right now, in our Fail Proof System, you are taking big, bold actions by diving into the deep end of your goals. With that, you're going to naturally encounter some failing moments! Those failing moments may be accompanied by strong emotions like frustration, shame, nerves, inadequacy, worry, embarrassment, and insecurity. This happens to all of us, but not all of us experience them, manage them, and act upon them in a way that truly serves us—and that's what makes all the difference. Let's develop your ability to respond rather than react, so that when most people stop, you keep going.

We're not robots. Well, not yet. Not until some tech billionaire rolls out the new line of eco-friendly cyborgs. We're humans, and in this human experience, we're given this wealth, depth, and range of human emotions. Some emotions are loving, connecting, and enriching. Others can be volatile, divisive, and destructive. And you've got them all, you lucky duck! So do I. We may at times wish we didn't, but we most certainly do. And just like with our quirky and sneaky brains, our emotions play by their own rules too.

We're never going to rid ourselves of emotions, nor should we. Not only are they a beautiful part of this complex life, but emotions are a powerful tool if we can channel them in the right way. They may even be a superpower. Just like a fire can warm your home or burn your house to the ground, emotions can help or harm us, depending on how we use them. Frankly put, you either control your emotions or your emotions control you. When making yourself Fail Proof, the objective is to observe, manage, and be the leader of your emotions. For yourself and the people who depend on you.

> you either control your emotions or your emotions control you.

When my emotions have gotten the better of me, it's shown itself in two different results. The first is big, grand fireworks. I am my father's son, and just like him, my intense love can sometimes be misguided. I know that in some of my early romantic relationships, small disagreements would devolve into full-fledged arguments and end with me doing dramatically over-the-top gestures to prove my unending affection. Like stopping traffic in the middle of a Manhattan crosswalk to proclaim my love for my girlfriend who's in the back of a taxi (poor girl was just trying to distance herself). Drama. King. No surprise I was drawn to the performing arts. I think back to those times, and I wasn't in control of my emotions. I was that emotion. I wasn't Alex; I was frustration, heartbreak, and fear in a six-foot body. Well, five-foot eleven if you want to be technical. I probably could have just taken a breath, acknowledged my piece in the disagreement, spoken with understanding and clarity, and we would have moved on about our day without all the crosswalk Shakespeare. But I did not possess the ability to manage my emotions, and so my surrounding work, relationships, and life suffered.

The other way my emotions have gotten the better of me is not with big, grand fireworks, but with quiet disengagement. Meaning, I will simply shrink away just like that teenager trying to disappear. I told you, emotions are sneaky, and they try to take control in different ways. We can feel our emotions, but we can't let them grab the steering wheel of how we think, speak, and act.

Can you recall a time in your life when emotions got the better of you? How did it go? Were you thinking, speaking, and acting in a way that truly supported you, your well-being, and your goals—or did the emotions grab the wheel? Think about those times and ask yourself: how might it have gone if you were in control? And more so, how might that have impacted what happened next in your life?

Mindfulness is growing in popularity, as it should be. A study by Massachusetts General Hospital shows that in eight weeks of practicing mindfulness you can improve your emotional regulation, learning, memory, and even positively change your brain.[10] But sometimes the term "mindfulness" can make us feel like we need to sit cross-legged, meditating with incense while we clutch crystals and bathe in essential oils. Now, I do support all that, but the truth is that mindfulness is simply the practice of observing. Observe the present moment and do so without judgment. By doing that, we are gifting ourselves so much autonomy, strength, and power. Mindfulness is awareness and an understanding that things don't just happen. There is a cause and an effect to everything.

"Between stimulus and response there is a space. In that space is our power to choose our response. In our response lies our growth and our freedom," said Viktor Frankl, a neurologist and Holocaust survivor. "Stimulus" is a fancy word for "things are going to happen." There will be things that happen that cause you to feel intense emotions: you hit a roadblock in your goal, get into an argument with someone you love, or get saddled with a colleague who always drops the ball on an important deadline. There is a difference between reacting and responding. Reacting is visceral, immediate, and intense. We think of a destructive thought, and we blurt out something horrible or act in a way that we will regret. Different than reacting, a response has more poise and tact. We feel the emotion occurring within us, but rather than immediately engaging with it, we manage the emotion and then think, speak, and act in a way that serves our greater interests.

Simply put, your emotions can be in the car, but they can't grab the steering wheel.

The Fail Proof System exists to make you unstoppable, and emotions are endless waves that can knock you to the ocean floor. But in the words of mindfulness expert, Jon Kabat-Zinn: "You can't stop the waves, but you can learn how to surf."

Well, surf's up. Here are my four vital keys for controlling your emotions so they don't control you:

1. You are not your emotions

Raise your hand if you've ever been told to hide your emotions, lock them up, or "tough it out"? I can't see you, but I know you're raising your hand, and I am too. Here's the thing. Emotions need to be processed, digested, and released. If we don't, we're just going to lug that big weight with us. It'll even feel like we're hauling "baggage." Emotions are meant to be felt. Feel them, but then allow them to move on without them taking control of you.

> **Just like you are not every thought you have, you are not every emotion you have either. It is not a life sentence. You can feel an emotion and then let that wave go. Maybe even observe and explore why you feel the way you do.**

Sometimes I'll get bummed out because I finished my favorite shrimp tacos. Then I realize I'm bummed out because I finished shrimp tacos, and maybe this doesn't deserve a full-on mood swing. Once we activate that muscle of awareness, I bet you'll start to have a good laugh at some of the causes that can result in emotional reactions. I'm not suggesting you become robotic or even stoic. I'm suggesting that you become aware of how you feel, why you feel that way, and then choose to think, speak, and act with your interests in mind rather than the interests of the emotion. This is how you become a dependable, consistent, and effective leader for yourself and the people who rely on you.

2. Snapbacks

We have our intense emotions, and we have our calming emotions. We have the sympathetic nervous system that triggers "fight or flight" and then the parasympathetic nervous system that calms, regulates, and relaxes.[11] There is a time and place for both. However, sometimes in our modern-day lives, the emotional reactions are a bit overboard for what happened. Meaning if you get rejected by a client, or you take the lead on a project and it's falling behind, or your idea for date night of playing giant Jenga gets shot down—you may feel a survival emotion kick in with strength. At your core, you are concerned about your well-being and how this setback will impact you, so the emotion is not invalid. But emotions can get carried away and cause us to do, say, or think things that hurt us and others. Maybe it becomes a horrible interaction with your client, team member, or loved one. Maybe the setback causes such an intense emotional reaction that it causes you to quit on your project, your job, or your relationship.

Here is where you need to manage your emotions and use a snapback—quite literally something to snap you back into the present moment and out of the whirlwind of that intense emotion or negative thought spiral. The good news is that there are endless ways to accomplish this if we're paying attention. You can count to twenty by odd numbers, snap your fingers while focusing on the physical sensations, breathe deep and extend the exhale, walk thirty steps and count your left foot touching the ground, shake out your body like a golden retriever leaving the water. That one feels less weird if you put on fun music and make it a dance. You can even focus your attention on a blade of grass, the texture of your desk, or a skin crinkle on your hand—which is also a great reminder to moisturize.

The key here is to snapback into the current moment and out of your intense negative emotions. When you do that, you can then refocus your attention on the present moment and the forward behaviors that will actually support you.

3. The *Net Positive* Perspective

You are not going to be positive all the time. That's impossible and honestly a little delusional. You'd have to be a unicorn born on a cupcake co-parented by Santa and the Tooth Fairy. It's just not realistic to always be in a good mood and be optimistic. That's an unreasonable request, and besides, we have negative emotions for a reason. To the points above, you can and should feel these emotions. They will give you character growth, grit, empathy, and strength. But here's the key.

> We become what we are most often. Meaning, if your default energy is negative, then you and your life will be negative. But if your default is positive energy, then you and your life will be powerhouses of positive energy too.

Here's a strategy I use daily: aim for a net positive. We are going to feel negative, neutral, and positive throughout the day. When you have a neutral, be neutral. When you have a positive, be positive. When you have a negative, the goal is to make it neutral. I would never ask you to turn a negative into a positive immediately; that's a lofty change-up, and if we can't do it, we'll tumble right back into negativity. But a very accomplishable goal is to notice when you are feeling down and simply ask yourself, "could I be neutral?" Meaning, can you not beat the crud out of yourself or get sucked into the what-if wasteland. Just be neutral.

I find this to be freeing, empowering, and most of all, do-able! Without the Net Positive Perspective, we might have an incredible morning, but a rough afternoon and a blah evening. Well, that scorecard is going to be even, or more likely, negative. But with the Net Positive Perspective, it just takes one positive moment to make it a positive day. In reality, your day is filled with so many micro-moments—you don't have a morning; you have one thousand little moments. So, all you need to do is monitor when you start to feel negative and see if you can feel the emotion but then course correct to even. Balanced. Neutral.

Why this is so powerfully impactful is that if you look at your scorecard at the end of the day: your positives will be positive, your neutrals will be neutral, and your negatives will be neutral. Meaning you've had a Net Positive day. If you do that, just imagine the compounding effect over time. Net Positive moments lead to Net Positive days, weeks, months, and a Net Positive life.

4. The Response-Time Variable

This is especially critical as you move closer to your goals because you will face tough emotions as you grow, learn, and improve. Now, think of an experience where you felt a strong emotion. After some time, that emotion subsided and went away. But how long that process takes is the variable. More specifically, how long that emotion keeps you from re-engaging productively for yourself and the people who need you—that's the variable we're talking about in the Fail Proof System. What if you didn't lose weeks, days, or even hours from a setback? What if you could immediately move through the emotions with ease and get right back to what matters to your well-being and success? What if you did that over and over again with all of the big and little setbacks that occur? Imagine the time, energy, and resources you'd save and how they could compound your results. When you hit a setback or adversity or failing, use these keys here to expedite the process of getting back to what matters most. Time is a variable, and this is how you take charge to make it your competitive edge.

Don't let emotions be in the driver's seat of your thoughts, words, and actions. Don't even let them be backseat drivers or fiddle with the radio. Emotions can be the passengers who sit quietly—and only if they bring snacks and gas money. You are in the driver's seat. You keep control of how you think, speak, and act, especially in moments of adversity, pressure, and uncertainty. Do that, and you'll forever change your life for the better.

Fail Proof Keys:

» Emotions are a beautiful part of this complex life, and can be a powerful tool if we channel them in the right way.

» Right now, and moving forward, be aware of your emotions, and try these tools & techniques:

  o Accept your emotion and also allow that wave to move on without immediately acting upon it.

  o Snapback into the present moment so you can think, speak, and act in a way that best serves you.

  o Make your negatives neutral and have a Net Positive life.

» Responding, rather than reacting, is one of the biggest differentiators of success. Do this and it will forever change your life for the better!

Step 5. Find Your Golden Nugget: Uncover Your Clues To Improvement

"When you fail, you figure it out. Frustration is the scent of learning."
—Callie Russell, Top Survivalist on *Alone*, 99 Days in the Wild

If we fail, then chances are there's something that we can do better. But it's not always easy to find this hidden clue of improvement. In fact, most people miss it. When most people hit a failing, they can summon the determination to give it another "go," but it's the same "go." The next attempt is usually very similar to the attempt that failed. So the determination ends up dying out because the progress dies out. This is why it's so valuable to be able to identify a takeaway from any failing. And not just any takeaway but an *actionable* takeaway. When we do that, it's worth its weight in gold.

Now, as we've discussed, when we face any setback, our emotions are going to kick up, and they'll attempt to distract us away from identifying this key piece of intel. So first off, kudos to you on managing that emotional reaction and responding in a better way. This right here is how we respond in that better way.

> **Failing is not forever. If we learn from each attempt, then we will improve until we no longer label it failing, we label it succeeding.**

Right now, we must be diligent to harvesting these clues to improvement.

In 2003, there was a mobile gaming company by the name of Relude. In their first six years, Relude brought fifty-one different games to market, yet none of these hit any real popularity or return. The company became low on resources, tight on money, and by 2009 was closing in on bankruptcy. In the final month of that year, the company rolled out its fifty-second game. Fifty-second. And as the former CEO, Pekka Rantala, says, "that fifty-second game in December 2009 really changed everything." It was a mobile game based upon feathered flying creatures of a rather moody disposition. Perhaps you've heard of it: *Angry Birds*. It seemed to have caught a resonance with people, as it became one of the most popular mobile games ever, blossomed to a movie, TV series, merchandise; and the company is valued at $1 billion with over 400 employees worldwide. Fifty-two attempts. The first attempt was not *Angry Birds*. It took each and every single one of those failed attempts to arrive at their winning formula.

And that's what this is all about: identifying your winning formula. We can find bits of your formula in research, books, and asking others for guidance, but there is no substitute for experience. There is no substitute in the formula for rolling up your sleeves and getting a little dirty. That's why I think of it as the golden nugget. You are out there in the mountains, hiked down to the river basin, waded out in the water, got muddy with these failed attempts, and as you do, you are mining for these valuable clues to the winning formula. After each and every attempt, you have uncovered a golden nugget—an actionable takeaway that when you put it to work will improve your performance and results. It's why I genuinely want you to take pride in the sheer fact that you are giving your best to these attempts. The true win is your continuing growth. When you do have a failed attempt, do not let your negative emotions rob you of this golden nugget. That would be like going out to the mountains, hiking down to river basin, wading in the water, getting muddy with these failed attempts, finally mining and finding a golden nugget—and then throwing it back. Keep your poise, and in the moments of setbacks, challenge yourself to identify the actionable takeaway. You earned it! And gosh, you look good in gold.

At times, it will be obvious what we can do better. But other times, we will get swept up in the whirlwind of what we're doing, and we'll fall into that trap of repeating our failing efforts. We're like that roaming, mechanical vacuum, Roomba, and we got caught ramming ourselves into a corner. The golden nugget is our way of redirecting that Roomba-like effort out of the dead end, and into the wide-open success of the living room carpet. Go, Roomba, go!

The vital key is recognizing this opportunity and mining for the golden nugget. As your performance improves, the golden nuggets will be less drastic and in-your-face—which is a great thing. But it also means we really need to challenge ourselves to continue to look for these places of improvement.

If we don't, we may very well make large strides in the beginning (because we had a lot of room for improvement!), but then our progress will stagnate and plateau as we become complacent and stop searching for the golden nuggets.

I know that in my pursuits, my desire and work ethic is there, but sometimes my emotions—whether enthusiasm or frustration—will get a hold of me after a failure, and I'll immediately want to just get right back to it! But the next failure quickly reminds me of that simple truth, "oh right, if I failed, then there's something I can do better. What is it?" We may need to even dig below the surface-level results and ask ourselves, "Why did this not go well?" Why did this meeting, or date, or competition, or sales presentation not go as we hoped? In any fail, micro or macro, if you can identify one actionable takeaway, it will elevate your performance each and every time. Find your golden nuggets, and before long, it'll be a full-on gold rush.

EMBRACE EACH STEP

You're on the journey here to becoming good at something—proficient, a high-performer, maybe even a pro. With that, we must learn, and grow, and improve to get there.

Many people become good at something early on in their lives. That period of learning, growing, and improving was done when it felt like less of a struggle—childhood. My pal Jake had skis strapped to his feet when he was two years old and can now jump out of helicopters to lay fresh tracks on mountaintops. My other buddy, Steve, just started learning to ski as an adult, and when I asked him how it was going, he promptly replied, "Do you know where I can sell my skis?" As kids, we're more okay with struggling to become good, because we're not harshly evaluating ourselves yet—and even if we did get frustrated, there was a teacher, parent, or authority encouraging us to keep doing it. But as adults, we don't allow ourselves to struggle at something. We're grownups! We have reputations to uphold and a LinkedIn profile to polish, for crying out loud. We can't struggle at something publicly. Nor do we want to force ourselves to struggle in private.

You've got to remember that realizing your goal is a process of small steps, and you *will* progress through each and every one. So rather than try to skip steps, or endure steps, what if you embrace each step? Knowing that even if this step is difficult or a little uncomfortable, before too long, you will become capable at it, and then be off to the next step. That next step may also be difficult and a little uncomfortable, but you'll have become accustomed to that sensation, and it'll stop feeling like as big of a deal. As the US Navy Seals say, "get comfortable being uncomfortable." Embracing each step is the way to do that.

What's even more empowering is that there is a pivotal threshold that we will hit. Let's say you were learning a new operating system at work, or focusing on a healthier diet, or trying to build a habit of meditating in the morning. It might be frustrating in the beginning as you strain to get the hang of it, and quitting might sound tempting because frankly put, you're not good at this yet. But if you simply commit through this period of difficulty, frustration, and discomfort—knowing that it is finite—then soon you will improve enough to the point that it is actually a little enjoyable to do it. You're still learning, growing, and building your skills, but it's less painful once you're half-way decent. You might even get a little excited to show off your progress to someone, "Hey Joyce! Check me out on this new spreadsheet!" You'll start to look forward to it and embrace the process because you're kind of enjoying it now. When this happens, you're off to the races.

No matter what you're trying to reach, challenge yourself to stick it through to this threshold.

> **The beautiful truth is that anything in this entire world is learnable—if you're willing to give your best, manage your emotions, mine for your golden nugget, and then, keep going.**

How amazing is that?! Anything you want to do in this world, you absolutely can do it. Will it be overwhelming, daunting, and frustrating at first? Oh, yes. Ten out of ten. But will that end? Yes. When it does, you'll be doing something you thought was impossible.

Remember, no matter your age, abilities, job title, or what's happened to you up to this point, there is nothing off-limits for you in this world if you are willing to commit. Let that sink in and allow your heart to expand with the beautiful possibilities that are unlocked for you.

The next chapter is all about how you commit to you—and how to keep going in the times when you want to stop.

Fail Proof Keys:

» In any fail, identify one actionable takeaway. Don't let emotions rob you of this valuable golden nugget.

» Embrace each step of your progress knowing that you will soon be through it and off to the next one.

» Everything is learnable. If you do embrace each step and commit to the progression, then nothing is off-limits for you in this world.

Step 6. Fully Commit (Again)

*"Most people fail, not because of a lack of desire,
but because of a lack of commitment."*

—Vince Lombardi, Five-Time NFL Champion Coach, Hall of Famer

Commitment dictates success. More accurately, your commitment dictates your success. Anything worthwhile, impressive, meaningful, and long-lasting requires overcoming difficult moments that test your commitment. So, the question is not only how you commit to your Fail Proof goals, but how do you commit to yourself?

> *your commitment dictates your success.*

There is an expression, "get knocked down seven times, get back up eight." But what about when you get knocked down the eighth time? Or the ninth time? Commitment is that will to stand back up no matter what, for yourself, and for the people who need you.

I believe this with every fiber of my being: **there is nothing more powerful than a person who really wants something**. When you really want something, there is no force on Earth that will keep you away from doing everything you can to make it happen. Think of a time in your life when you wanted something (or someone) so badly that it kept you awake at night. Did you do bold things? I bet you did. I used to write love poems to my high school girlfriend. And by "girlfriend," I mean a cool senior girl I had a massive crush on for years. She turned me down, but I was unfazed; I just kept sending more mediocre poems.

When you really want something, you will make it happen. You will find a way. For yourself and for the people who need you.

YOUR POWERFUL WHY

Right now, we're going to check in with ourselves and get clear on the visceral reason why you want this for yourself, your life, and the people in it. I call this "Your Powerful Why," and it goes way beyond the outcome of your Fail Proof goals. It's the reason your goal makes your heart beat faster. As much as I want the buzzer in *American Ninja Warrior* (and I do!), I train and compete because it makes me feel alive. At my core, my deepest driving reason is that I want to prove to myself that I can do anything even if I have doubts. I want to show myself that I am capable of doing things that I once believed were impossible, and I can succeed where I've failed over and over again.

For my entire life, being an athlete has been my source of identity, purpose, passion, and fulfillment. Then after college lacrosse—hard stop. I still remember that first time someone referred to me as a "former athlete." It felt like a drop kick to my soul. When *American Ninja Warrior* hurdled into my life, it also hurled me back into being an athlete, even with all the failings. Now, as I train and compete, I'm accomplishing feats that I couldn't do when I was a twenty-one-year-old Division I athlete. It makes me feel like age is just a number, and I'm more alive now than I ever have been. It makes me feel like I can still surprise myself, and that I can do anything, even if I've failed at it. And if I do that, then I can help other people do it too! All of that is my Powerful Why. Is it intense? Maybe. But you know what else is intense? Goals. That's why having something powerful inside of you during the moments you're challenged is invaluable. We all need to call upon it in our toughest moments, those moments where we may be tempted to quit on ourselves and the people who need us. This is your firepower.

So, what is your Powerful Why? Think about it. Really dive into the meaning you have for this goal. Both right now, and what it may bring to your future. Poke around and explore. Keep asking yourself, "Okay, but why?" until you get down to the simple, driving, visceral reason. That's your Powerful Why.

I'll never forget that night in Las Vegas where I almost gave up on myself—and I needed my Powerful Why. It was at the end of that second season hosting for NBC *American Ninja Warrior*, where my bosses—the producers—had asked me to become good at this incredibly difficult sport. Our series finale was at the National Finals course, where the top American Ninja Warrior athletes from all across country compete on the final, most intense stages of the competition. One of the producers came to me and said, "Alex, we have an opportunity for you to try the newest, most dynamic"—that means difficult—"new obstacle, and we're going to have all of the television cameras on you, the audience will be packed, and we'll have one chance to do this." Huh. Packed audience, TV cameras, the most dynamic (difficult) new obstacle. And one chance?

The day leading up to it, my negative voice of fear was really shining bright. It was like a karaoke night of greatest hits. "What if you fail?" "One chance! Did you hear that?" "Real Ninja Warriors have a tough time on this obstacle, and you're not even a real athlete anymore." My negative voice wasn't holding back. In fact, it started to plant some excuses in my mind. "You feel that tickle in your throat? You're sick, and you can't do it." "Pitch them on an idea where instead of doing the obstacle. You...don't...." "This is Vegas, just disappear! Maybe you could work in a magic show." Here's the thing. The producers would never make me do this feat; this was completely up to me. If anything, they were thrilled to be able to offer me this incredible opportunity—because it *is* an incredible opportunity. But all my negative fear voice could see is all of the horrible possibilities that may or may not happen. It was forcing me to put on these awful glasses where that's the prescription: negativity and fear.

I had a bravely honest moment with myself. "Alex, you don't have to do this. If you don't want to do it, then don't. But if you do want to do it, then do it. So...do you want to do it? What does this mean to you?"

"Well, Alex," I said to myself, "thanks for asking. I love this job, I love this sport, I love this community, and it makes me feel alive. It pushes me to do things that I didn't think I could do." I paused. "Exactly like this opportunity tonight."

> **You see, my negative voice was so loud that it blinded me from the truth, and worse, it was trying to rob me of everything I actually loved.**

I decided in that moment to commit to myself. I showed up that night—still with the nerves, still with the doubt, still with the fear—but I chose to not listen to that voice. Instead, I chose to believe in myself. As I walked on set, I told myself, "all you can do is the best you can do."

The obstacle I'd be facing is called the "Double Dipper." It rises three stories in the air. This is the Vegas National Finals after all; everything is bigger! To begin the obstacle, you grab on to a bar that is free sliding on a rollercoaster-like contraption. As you hold onto the bar, the rest of your body free dangles in the air. The bar—with you dangling off of it—then shoots down the twenty-foot slide to an abrupt stop, where you're then catapulted, free flying in the air to yet another bar that is free sliding on yet another rollercoaster like contraption. It's a doozy! Athletically and technically very difficult. Awesome.

"Alex, we're ready for you," the producer said. "Wow, okay here we go." I stepped up to the massive forty-foot-high obstacle. I literally had to be mindful of each step as I climbed up onto this behemoth. I finally get up there, look over, and yup, the audience is packed! They're cheering as the first camera swoops in on cables and pulleys. "Woah, they're not messing around," I thought. My internal dialogue's running. "Yowzer, this is high up. Okay, Alex, just focus on what you need to do.

Hold the bar with a mix grip so you don't slip off, try to feel out the descent, and make sure your legs are kicked back so that when the hard stop happens you have momentum, then keep your legs tucked, grab the second bar up high with a mix grip so that the drop doesn't rip you off—wait, smile for the camera, that's part of your job too!" It's A LOT!

The next camera passes as a huge gust of wind comes in. We're in Las Vegas, and off the strip, it's still the desert! "Okay that was a little chilly, just keep staying loose, stay ready." This is a televised competition, and you need to be ready to go when it works in the television production. There is no "just give me a second." I'm looking down at the course-producer. It's hard to make him out because it's so dang high on the obstacle, but I know when he gives me the hand signal, it's time to rock—okay, there it is!

It is go time. In this moment, I do what I always do in any big moment: focus on what I need to do. Then I take a deep breath, choose to believe in myself, and let it fly! BIG, BOLD ACTION. No holding back, full commitment, no regrets. All you can do is the best you can do.

I grab the bar with my hands in a mix grip. The bar starts its slide, slow at first, then it hits the tipping point and shoots down, my body shooting with it. I try to navigate my legs, but we're going too fast, and boom—the bar hard stops. I'm free flying like a human slingshot. Tuck the legs, mix grip, grab the bar high, whoosh the second slide hurdles down then hard stops, shooting me off again. I go flying in the air one more time, spot the landing mat, and—thwat! It's done. I made it. I did it.

> **After failing for two years straight on every obstacle I touched, I succeeded on the Las Vegas National Finals Course of NBC *American Ninja Warrior* with a packed audience, TV cameras, and with my voice of negativity telling me I couldn't do it. I will never forget that moment. It unlocked the truth to me.**

The truth that if you are willing to commit to yourself, if you are willing to embrace failing, then there is no stopping what you can do. You will accomplish feats you thought were impossible. You will be unstoppable.

I want you to think about your Fail Proof goals, and I want you to think about what they really mean to you. Not just the surface level result, but what accomplishing that result truly means to you. Remember, that is your firepower.

Maybe it's that someone told you that you couldn't do it, but you're the one who decides what you do. Maybe it's that you've always wanted to do this, but fear and life and other people's judgments have gotten in the way. Well, not anymore! Now you are honoring yourself. Maybe it's that you want to be the reason that other people succeed. I'm getting a little fired up writing these! Your answer is your answer—there is no right or wrong. If it gets your heart beating and makes you want to go and do this, well then there it is. *Ding, ding,* we have a winner! Your Powerful Why is the positive energy furnace churning inside of you.

> **When you decide that you really want something, when you decide to commit to yourself no matter what—there is nothing that will keep you from it. You are unstoppable.**

Now one more tactical note. Suppose you've done your best, chosen to believe in yourself, and then you fall short. You fail. It can be hard to believe that your next attempt will be any different. I've emphasized the importance of managing emotions, but we also need to embrace our emotions too. You are not a robot, so rather than trying to be one, or treating your emotions as a liability, let's make them an asset. Emotions are energy. No one has ever said, "I'm so nervous, I could take a nap!" No. Emotions activate your body. They fire up your system. You are alert. In fact, research out of Harvard Business School shows being nervous and being excited are simply a matter of perspective, and one that we can alter with our outlook.[12] This is yet another power of being positive about yourself and what you're doing. If we can harness our emotions, we can turn them from a weakness to a strength. If you're frustrated, annoyed, ticked off, nervous, or excited, use the energy. How do we use it? Channel it toward your golden nuggets. You have your arsenal of actionable takeaways. If you keep using them, you can trust that your results will improve. Use your emotional fuel, implement your actionable takeaway, fully commit, and you will do better. Rinse, and repeat.

Here is the breakdown of the Fail Proof System:
1. Get clear on your goal and what it means to you.
2. Start. Build your momentum.
3. Dive in the deep-end with big, bold actions.
4. Harness your emotional response.
5. Learn an actionable takeaway.
6. Fully commit again with big, bold action.

Now, within this system, there is an incredible opportunity to hyperdrive your progress.

Once you are clear on your goal and your Powerful Why (Step 1), you make this goal real (Step 2), and you've taken big, bold action (Step 3)—you've now entered the hyperdrive stage, because Steps 4–6 can be on repeat. You take big, bold action, you manage your emotions, learn an actionable takeaway, and then fully commit again with big, bold action—and the cycle continues. This is the recipe. But some people are unable to bake the cake, or they take forever to do it, or they get so frustrated that they leave the kitchen altogether. Not you, this is your quick-fire sequence to cook up success in record time.

People quit on themselves and their goals because their emotions overpower them, they don't challenge themselves to focus on improvements, and they are unclear of why this commitment matters to them. The results suffer, the desire dwindles, and eventually, they stop. But not you. You have this Fail Proof System. You have the tools to manage your emotions and channel them for good. You have the ability to identify ways to keep learning, growing, and improving. And you have the clarity on your Powerful Why so you will keep committed. You are the complete package.

And one more thing: Celebrate your little wins along the way, wouldya! They're not all going to be massive, monumental, ticker-tape parades, nor should they be. That's what you're building toward, and along the way, you want to take genuine pride in your progress. Learning a new skill, pitching an idea with confidence, putting on that shirt that used to feel shrunk but now you feel like a million bucks. Feel that, and allow it to resonate in you. Momentum is real. Fuel yourself with positive energy, keep fully committed, over and over again, and you will be unstoppable.

Fail Proof Keys:

» What's your Powerful Why? What is your visceral motivator? Why are you doing this?

» If you keep committed to yourself and embrace failing, then there is no stopping what you can do.

» There is a hyperdrive in this system.
  o Big, bold action.
  o Use your emotional fuel.
  o Implement your golden nugget.
  o Fully commit again with big, bold action. Rinse, and repeat—and you will get to your goal.

FAIL PROOF RESILIENCE: BEING UNSTOPPABLE

Give Your Best To Receive The Best: The Unexpected Gifts

"It's not about the forty seconds; it's about the four years, the time it took to get there."
—Apolo Ohno, Eight-Time Olympic Medalist in Speed Skating

> **Our fifth promise is being open to all the unexpected gifts that will come to your life—the growth, the people, the experiences, and the opportunities—even in our darkest moments, where we don't think it's possible.**

You can always find my mom in the kitchen—she's Italian after all! She just wants to feed you, hug you, and love you. She makes a mean chicken piccata, and every time I'm home, she cooks it for me because it's my favorite. I can't help but smile watching her do it. She has so much joy and energy cooking it up. She buzzes around the kitchen with pure excitement to feed her son his favorite dish. It's beautiful.

But this day was different. I had gone upstairs to wash up for dinner, and when I came down, the house didn't smell like lemon piccata magic; it smelled like a burning pan. Instead of seeing my mom buzzing around the kitchen, chopping, and stirring with joy, she was standing over the counter, still and silent. Just staring down. I went over to her and put my hand on her shoulder. She slowly looked up at me, and her face said everything before she spoke.

Have you ever known that life as you know it is about to change forever?

I've only seen my mom cry twice in my life. Once, when her father passed, and then this moment. I hugged her as she cried in my arms, and it was tough to make out what she was saying, but I could piece together the words "rare," "stage four," and "cancer."

I love my mom very much. Maybe it was the fact that I was an Accident Kid, but she and I have always seemed to have a special connection. Case in point, she never called me an accident (my dad and sister playfully did). She always called me her unexpected gift. What a sweet lady, right?! She's pure good on this planet, and here she was hurting. *Really hurting.* She's in pain, and she's scared, and I'm scared for her. Real fear. And I had no idea what to do. I felt completely out of control.

THE UNCONTROLLABLES

How many things are outside of your control?

Make a list.

Start with the weather. Then hop over to politics. Then to your colleague's actions. Or that specific thing someone you love does that you've talked with them about, and they said they'd stop doing it, but wouldn't you know it, here they are doing it again.

Make a list of all the things that are outside of your control. I'll wait.

1.

2.

3.

4.

5.

6.

7.

8.

9—okay, that'll eat up your whole day.

If it seems like there are endless things outside of our control, it's because there *are* endless things outside of our control. And yet, these things impact you profoundly. They affect your success, fulfillment, and well-being. They influence your life and the people in it, and you have no say over any of them.

It can be incredibly daunting and make us feel powerless—like we're trying to play dodgeball, but we don't have any balls on our side of the court. And we're looking over at our opponents, who are all-star pitchers with over-inflated kickballs ready for a firing squad!

Whizzz! The world's being crazy.

Whoosh! People are being crazy.

Zing! My job is being crazy, and my life is being crazy, and you know what, I might be crazy too!

There will always be endless things outside of your control impacting your success, fulfillment, and well-being. Things you don't have a say in, will never have a say in, and often don't even know will happen! But there is also one thing that is always within your control: You. Which means that you matter.

You matter.

I'm going to say that again: *You matter.* Maybe you need to hear that right now. Maybe you don't think you do, but you do. Or there might be a time in the future where you need to remind yourself of this simple truth that you matter.

> **Maybe someone or something has tried to convince you that you are not of impact, not of consequence, that you can be overlooked or ignored. They're wrong.**

There are causes and effects in this world, and you are a cause. We all want results. Results are the realization of our Fail Proof goals: money in the bank, deals closed, incredible nights shared with the person you love most, and looking yourself in the mirror with a deep sense of pride in who you've become.

Results are amazing. But we can't touch them right now. You cannot touch the results. The results are over in a *Museum of The Future*, in a glass case, with a velvet rope around it, protected by a security guard named Karl who's got a giant taser and will zap you if you get close. The only thing that you can touch are these moments right now and what you put into them. So then the question becomes: What do you put into life?

GIVE THE GAME THE BEST YOU HAVE

My high school bio teacher was named Dr. Fiorella, but between you and me, I don't think he was a doctor. I think he just liked the nickname. You ever have someone in your life who just really wants a nickname? Like someone who wants to be called "Captain," and you're like, "You can't even drive a car, Sam." Well, we just threw Dr. Fiorella a bone on this one.

Dr. Fiorella was a very interesting guy. He was my freshman year running coach and biology teacher. He was a sweet, quiet man, but here's the unique part: he was also a Golden Glove boxer, which is one of the highest ranks you can receive in combat sports!

Every week, he would hang on the wall one of his life philosophies. He would call them "Dr. Fiorella's 'Fio-losophies.'" He was quite pleased with himself about that.

There was one Fio-losophy that I loved. Dr. Fiorella knew I loved it too, and at the end of the year, he signed it and gave it to me as a gift. It's still on my desk to this day—in fact, I'm looking at it right now. It says, "Give the game the best you have, and the best will come back to you."

Now at the time, as a sports-obsessed teenager whose dream it was to play college lacrosse, this was pretty on the nose. The game. Sports! Dr. Fio gets it! It wasn't until much later that I learned "the game" is much bigger than sports. The game is anything that you decide to care about. Again, nothing matters except what you choose matters. So "the game" is anything that you decide matters to you: matters to your work, matters to your relationships, matters to your life.

What I love about this philosophy is that it starts with "give." It begins with you stepping up to contribute to your life. Remember: you matter. You are of impact. You get a say. And what do you give to life? What's your contribution to the game?

Your best.

No small task! Certainly not. It's a pretty tall order indeed. But if you decide to step into your life and give the best of yourself—your thoughts, your words, and your actions—then guess what you'll receive in return: *the best.*

Here's an important clarification. It does not say, "Give the best you have, and you will get your result." That would be a lie. That would require us to be those pointy-hat wizards capable of removing life's uncertainty and adversity from the equation, and that's not part of this beautiful life we get to live. But if you give the best you have, then the best will come back to you. So, what is the best?

UNEXPECTED GIFTS

You are committed to realizing the rewards of your Fail Proof goals: money in the bank, closed deals, special nights with the ones you love, and looking in the mirror at your best self. Our fifth promise is to be open to the wide-breadth of all the wonderful gifts that may come to you in pursuit of your goals. I believe these gifts come back to you in growth, people, experiences, and opportunities. And sometimes, the gifts are unexpected.

I didn't want my mom to get diagnosed with cancer. I didn't explore my life and decide on this goal. Life did what life does and threw a big old question mark of uncertainty and adversity our way. But we are focusing on what is in our control: us. And giving the best we have to this goal. Our Fail Proof goal is for her to be strong, healthy, and healed. But guess what else happened: our relationship grew and deepened in ways I never thought possible. An unexpected gift.

We've always had beautiful experiences together. A lot of our favorite times would be going for long walks while our little Yorkie pup, Bammer, scampered to keep up and then would get exhausted because her gallop stride is about three inches. So, we pick her up, put her in her carrier, and sneak her into a restaurant. There, my mom and I would split a healthy salad and a burger as a treat to celebrate our time together. It was fun! But, now, we've gone a layer deeper together.

We have a bond that is deeper in our hearts than walks or treats could ever do. Chemo beds will do that. We've been in treatment centers in various cities and even different countries when she couldn't get the treatments she needed. We've been scared together, we've made big decisions together, we've cried together, and even cried until we laughed together. Even though this is not what we wanted, we decided to give the best we had to it, and unexpected gifts have come back to us. And I'm grateful for them.

I want you to look at your life right now, the people in it, and any challenges you may be facing, and I want you to ask yourself: could there be an unexpected gift here?

Ask yourself: What might happen if you give your best? If you give the best you have, could you get the best back in return? Is it possible that unexpected gifts may come to you in the form of growth, people, experiences, and opportunities?

Nothing in this world is guaranteed, but I do assure you this: no gifts have ever come to those who quit. There will always be so many things outside of your control. But what you put into the game, what you give for yourself and the people who need you—that's entirely up to you. I have one question: Will you give your best?

Before you answer, think about your goals. Think about why you want them, what it means to you, and what it could mean to the people in your life. And if your answer is yes, you will give your best, then let's make it happen for you.

You have the system; you know our promises. Embrace it, commit to it, and you will be Fail Proof. You will be unstoppable.

Fail Proof Keys:

» When life is out of control, overwhelming, or daunting, focus on what you can put into life. Give your best to receive the best.

» Gifts come back to us in growth, people, experiences, and opportunities.

» If you are facing a challenge right now, could there be any unexpected gifts in it for you?

o Character growth, deepened connections, enriching experiences, or unseen opportunities?

15

Floats & Anchors: Stack Your Support

--- --- --- --- --- --- --- --- --- --- --- --- ---

"To honor life, we must be willing to grow through what we don't know yet, and outgrow what we know no longer fits us. We must be willing to give in to the process, moment by moment, realizing that a new plot may be unfolding."
—Iyanla Vanzant, Bestselling Author

You dove in the deep end (or a cannon ball, or jack knife, or belly flop) and you are in the water of what you want to do. You are swimming toward your goal, and even when you hit choppy waters, or avoid dangers, or knock into a buoy, or a piece of seaweed touches your leg, you are still committed to reaching your goal. As you do this all, there are going to be factors that lift you up or drag you down. I call them your floats and your anchors. The intention is to surround yourself with floats that lift you up, because swimming is tough enough, and the last thing you need are anchors weighing you down.

> **Floats are those things that make you better, and they come in many forms. They come in the form of actions. They come in the form of our inner voice. And they come in the form of people.**

Right now, there are probably people that pop in your head as human beings who lift you up. How cool is that?! Maybe they are supportive, maybe they challenge you, maybe they just love you for who you are right now. Maybe just knowing them makes you want to become a better version of yourself. Those people are floats. Now there are also people who are anchors. People who don't have your best interest at heart, don't challenge or support you, don't love you, and don't make you want to be the best version of yourself. I'm sure there's people who pop into your head for that too. Those people are anchors. We have floats and anchors in these different areas, and we want to stack your deck with support for being and becoming your best self.

YOUR ACTIONS

There are actions you take that serve to raise you up and make you a better version of yourself—and then there are some actions that don't. We're human, and we do both. No shaming here, but we should be bravely honest about the fact that not everything we do serves us and apply a bit of awareness to identify those behaviors that don't. Set your self-judgment aside and determine which of your activities support you or sabotage you.

For instance, there is a difference between self-care and self-destruction. Self-care is having your favorite glass of wine, relaxing to a movie, or getting a little bit extra sleep. Self-destruction is downing a bottle of wine, watching a movie marathon until 2:00 a.m., and pounding coffee nonstop the next morning to endure through your day.

What actions lift you up? Why? Go ahead and make a list. It can be simple actions like prepping before a meeting, calling an old friend for a laugh, or drinking water throughout the day. When we become clear on the actions that support us, we can then get really clear on how to foster them. For instance, I drink more water when I use a glass instead of a bottle. Weird, right? Believe me, I know. But it's true, and it works for me. That may seem like a benign detail, but if I drink from a glass, then I drink more water. If I drink more water, I have more energy, I'm healthier, I feel better, I look better, and I perform better. So, it's not really a benign detail, it's of consequence. Especially when we're talking about compounding and stacking our floats. This compound, stacking effect also occurs for the anchors. We're either going to be lifting ourselves up or dragging ourselves down with these actions, and it begins with keen awareness to which actions produce which results.

INNER VOICE

Your Inner Voice is comprised of your beliefs, your thoughts, and your words—both the ones you speak to yourself and the ones you speak to the world. As I mentioned earlier in this book, we have 70,000 thoughts a day, and 40,000 of them skew negative, which means our brains don't always have our back. You are not your brain, and you are not your fear. You do not need to listen to every opinion they tell you. You are going to have negative thoughts, emotions, and words because you are human. Be aware of them, and when you notice that they may not have your best interest at heart, course correct back to your positive energy voice. Use our tools and techniques from earlier chapters for fostering positive self-beliefs and managing your emotions (snapback, Net Positive, reframing negative beliefs). This is a muscle, and you will strengthen it. Your positive inner voice is about to get a six pack.

Whether you realize it or not, your outward voice comes from your inner voice, and it impacts your life, the people around you, and your surrounding world. Be mindful of the words that you speak. They last longer than the sounds they make.

> *Be mindful of the words that you speak. They last longer than the sounds they make.*

PEOPLE

Who you engage with in your life is a recurring pillar in this book, and for good reason. People can bring out the best of you. Amazing parts within you that maybe you weren't even sure you had. People can also bring out the worst in you too. But we have the freedom to choose who we give more of our moments. Look at the people in your work, in your relationships, and in your life and think, who lifts me up? Maybe there are people who, when you're with them, just make you feel better about yourself. Perhaps they hold you accountable, or they give you encouragement, or maybe even some honest, direct real talk when you need to hear it. *"I love you, but you need to wear less denim.*" If you're with someone, and they lift you up, they're a float!

I'm constantly in awe of how supportive the *American Ninja Warrior* community is to one another. Now it's not always feel-good hugs; sometimes it's challenging each other, or pushing one another forward, and those are all the wonderful shades of true support and true leadership. Who does that for you? There's no right or wrong here, but make a list of the floats and anchors in your life. Shine a bravely honest light on the people who support you—and also on the people who impede your well-being, fulfillment, and success. Don't worry, you can burn the list after, and they'll never see it. Although it might be nice to share with your floats.

Now, I want to address loyalty as well. Once you're aware that someone integral to your life is, in fact, an anchor, that can be a tough realization and difficult to navigate. Ultimately, it is up to you whether (and how) you keep that individual in your life. You can have a tactful, good-intentioned conversation with them sharing your experience in hopes of bettering the situation. But you also have every permission in this world to keep them at an arm's distance. A very long arm. My good friend, Dr. Gwynn, would always encourage me to do this. Well, I guess she's not technically my good friend. In her words, "Alex, I'm your therapist. It has been five years!" Classic Dr. Gwynn.

> **Establishing boundaries and barriers that protect your well-being, fulfillment, and success is a phenomenal act of self-leadership. This is not being disloyal; this is taking care of yourself. If you're able to take care of yourself, you'll be able to take care of other people as well. Remember, you need support, not impediments. You need floats, not anchors.**

As you go on this journey to your Fail Proof goals, keep focused on your floats and allow yourself the freedom to give more of your heartbeats to the actions, people, and inner voice that lift you up, and less to the ones that drag you down.

Now sometimes, floats can give you unexpected gifts. An incredible and hilarious occurrence proved this truth to me—and it has to do with a penguin.

It began with that special poster I had on my wall growing up. I first got it when I was a lacrosse-obsessed kid. That same kid who was getting bullied by Joey Lautner then became that same young man who cried in a bathroom stall, heartbroken and hiding his tears from his teammates. That poster of the World Championship of Lacrosse that my dad gave me. That poster that I would look at every day and dream of one day playing in the World Championship.

Winning US Lacrosse Coach of the Year in Los Angeles unlocked opportunities to play and coach internationally. Now, as I mentioned to you, I was invited to try out for the Argentinian National team as one of their three non-passport spots, and I was selected to go down to Argentina to compete in their National Championship before we'd head to Israel for the World Championship.

When I got to Argentina, I was staying with a teammate, Nico, in Patagonia. Nico didn't know much English, and I don't know much Spanish. I know a few years of high school Spanish, like "*Sophie va a la biblioteca.*" Let me tell you something: I was down there for a month; nobody went to the "*biblioteca.*" My Spanish was useless. Nico and I didn't have much of a connection, but also, it didn't matter to me at the time because I was so fixated on my singular goal: which was to actually score goals on the lacrosse field. I felt like I had a chance to finish the loop from the college player who underperformed, lost his dream, and cried in that stall. I had blinders on, and so I didn't care too much about forming bonds, I wanted to succeed at my singular goal. Until my last day with Nico. He came to me, and I could tell he spent time crafting this sentence. He said, "Alex, do you want to go to Penguin Beach?"

I replied, "What is Penguin Beach?"

Nico said, "It's a beach with forty thousand penguins."

I was speechless. Stunned. Also, a little peeved. I'd never seen a penguin before in my life. I sort of thought they weren't real. I said, "Nico. You're telling me there is a beach with forty thousand penguins…and we *weren't* going to go?! Let's get in the *coche*!"

So, Nico and I head to Penguin Beach, and I kid you not, there are forty thousand penguins. An impossible number of penguins. It's a nature preserve, so the penguins aren't afraid of humans either. They'll just waddle right up to you and adorably shove you out of their way. I was having a blast with the penguins, and I decided that I'd love to get a photo with one of them—a keepsake for this special memory (read: share on social media that I met a penguin). I waddled over to a particularly photogenic penguin to get a photo. Yes, I waddled too; do as the locals do, right? I pulled out my camera and stretched my arm out to do a selfie, but the penguin wasn't looking. It's tough to get the penguin to pose because—and not many people know this—penguins don't care about social media. To get its attention, I chirped out, "Penguin, penguin, penguin!" Then I remembered he speaks Spanish, so I corrected, "*Pinguino, pinguino, pinguino!*" Still no luck.

I inched closer, close enough to see the penguin flapping its wings a little through my camera's screen—an adorable warning sign, but a warning sign nonetheless. I'm so oblivious that all I can think is, "Wow, that's dynamic. Looking good, buddy!" I crouched down a bit lower to get my face in the frame with my tiny *pinguino amigo*, but as I did, my feet gave way and I slipped to the ground, startling the little one, and— it bit me. The penguin bit me on the finger! *Pinche pinguino!*

It didn't hurt at all, but it did rock my world. *Cute bully.* I dusted myself off and looked over to see Nico doubled over, laughing. As he should, since I just got beat up by a penguin. I see him laughing, I start laughing, and to this day, Nico and I are friends for life. And even though friendship wasn't my goal, that unexpected gift allowed me to perform better at achieving my goal. When I went to play on the lacrosse field, I would see Nico and my teammates, feel how much they meant to me, and I'd want to perform better for them. I said that caring about people is not an inconsequential afterthought, it's a better way of reaching results. Caring about my teammates and being open to gifts spurred me to finish as a top goal scorer in the World Championships of Lacrosse, and my organization had our best competition ever. All with a penguin bite on my finger.

Floats will not only lift up our performance, they will give us unexpected gifts with them. Growth, experiences, opportunities, and people (and sometimes penguins).

In our lives, we have floats and anchors.

I ask you, what might happen if you overload your life with floats? If your life is busting at the seams with support? What might be possible if you fill your life with the actions, people, and an inner voice that continually lift you up?

I imagine it might be like a scene from a comedy where someone is handed a balloon. Then another, and another, and another until they become a human hot-air balloon lifting far off into the sky. Why not do that? Why not stack every element you possibly can to support you and lift you up?

Start today. Start right now. You reading this book is a float activity. Follow it up with another. As you go through your days, keep asking: "does this lift me up or drag me down?" and as you do, give more and more of your heartbeats to what supports you. You're not going to be perfect at it, nobody is. But we are the product of what we do most often. So, if you continually surround yourself with floats that lift you up, then you are going to live an elevated life. You'll be amazed by the quality of your journey, you'll be amazed by the quality of your results, and you'll be amazed by the quality of your life.

Fail Proof Keys:

» There are floats and anchors—factors that lift you up or drag you down. These come in the form of actions, your inner voice, and people.

» Right now in your life, what are some floats and what are some anchors? Which ones are really impactful?

» How can you give more of your heartbeats to your floats, and less to your anchors?

16

Unstoppable Leadership

"Our greatest glory is not in never falling,
but in rising every time we fall."
—Confucius, Philosopher

In becoming Fail Proof, you have activated, embodied, and strengthened your leadership qualities. We've focused your Unstoppable Leadership on first leading yourself. Because if you want to authentically show up for other people, you need to authentically show up for yourself. At this point, you've sincerely done that. You've set clear goals that matter, given your best, and even in the setbacks—you're managing your emotions, improving, and keeping committed to your highest goals. You can now genuinely and effectively help other people do it too. True leadership. You can now set goals with others that matter, activate their self-belief and commitment, help manage their emotions to be used positively, and foster learning, growth, and improvement to achieve your highest goals together. Bravo! And remember, you do not need to be a finished, polished product. By giving your best to leading others, you will continually cultivate your highest self with it. Now, let's do it. Let's go full force on delivering this Unstoppable Leadership to all the people who need you.

YOU ARE A LEADER

Maybe you are a veteran leader, and you are excited for these insights and strategies for Unstoppable Leadership. Perhaps you're a new leader, unsure about stepping up for the first time into a leadership role. Maybe you don't think of yourself as a leader at all, never have, and you don't think you ever will be a leader. Well, to that, I say *nonsense*. We are all leaders, whether we realize it or not.

> **There will be times in your life where people look to you, where people depend on you, and where they need you to be at your best. That is leadership, and the opportunity will be there for you.**

This section is about leading in the toughest of times, when life doesn't care about your plans or goals. When life blindsides you with a whirlwind of uncertainty, changes, unknown future, and even tragedy, this is where we all need Unstoppable Leaders to step up. Unstoppable Leaders like the one you're about to become.

LEADING WITH RESILIENCE

You're doing everything right. You've set a goal that matters; you're committing to giving your best to what you can touch; you're using your emotions as positive fuel, continually learning, growing, improving, and fully recommitting even in the tough times. You're even starting to experience some of the wonderful benefits and unexpected gifts of this path. Then, life does what life does. You have a game-plan, but life has a plan of its own—plans that shake your industry, your job, and even your life.

I don't mean a brush back, a push back, or a setback. I mean when your life changes in an instant, and your world crumbles to the ground. When you have fear about your future, and the people who depend on you? They're scared too. How do you show up then as a leader for yourself and a leader for those who need you?

What if I were to tell you that it is those lowest lows that will lead you and your people to the highest highs? I gave a TEDx Talk on an astounding occurrence in our world. I noticed a unique pattern, and it has to do with the power of people in their darkest times.

I realized that after their cities are hit with devastating tragedies, the pro sports teams go on to win the championships. Interesting, no? Could there be a link between the two? And if so, how?

After Hurricane Katrina devastated New Orleans in 2005, the New Orleans Saints won the Super Bowl.

After Hurricane Harvey flooded Houston in 2017, the Houston Astros won the World Series.

After a tragic shooting in Las Vegas in 2017, the Vegas Golden Knights made it all the way to the Stanley Cup Finals in their very first season.

Hm. Maybe it's a coincidence.

In New York City, after the World Trade Center towers were attacked and collapsed, the New York Yankees advanced to the World Series, just barely losing in the final game seven.

After the Boston Marathon bombing, the Boston Red Sox won the World Series Championship, and the Boston Bruins went to the Stanley Cup Finals.

Okay, maybe this is just in the United States. We do love our sports, after all.

In 2011, there was a catastrophic tsunami and earthquake in Japan, and fifteen thousand people died. A devastating tragedy. Following this disaster, the Japanese Women's Soccer Team played in the World Cup. Before 2011, the team never even advanced out of the qualifying round. This means they didn't win enough games to even get into the tournament bracket. Following the 2011 tragedy, the Japanese team advanced out of qualifying and made it to the quarterfinals, where they competed against the host nation, perennial powerhouse and two-time World Cup defending champions, Germany. Japan was facing an absolute juggernaut. Germany had won the last two World Cups, and they are playing on German soil. Japan's loss was all but guaranteed. And yet, Japan won. The Japanese Women's team then convincingly defeated Sweden in the semifinals to advance to the World Cup Finals, a level of achievement they'd never reached before or even come close to reaching. But now they hit the brick wall, top-seed, and wildly favored USA. Japan trailed all through regulation time, but they were somehow able to battle back to tie the game and push to overtime in the final minutes. They trailed yet again in overtime, but somehow were able to tie the score in the closing minutes to push to penalty kicks. And in their sport's most intense moment on its biggest stage—*they won*. The Japanese Women's Soccer Team won their very first World Cup. They became the first Asian nation ever to win, and only the fourth nation overall to ever win the World Cup, beating the last two champions in the process. They accomplished all this, just months after their homes were buried under rubble, fifteen thousand of their people died, and their country experienced one of the most devastating heartbreaks humans can ever endure.

How?

How did they turn this horrific low into an incredible high? Where people were once holding one another crying tears of heartbreak, they're now holding one another with tears of joy. How did they do it? And how can you do it when you and those you care about face your toughest moments?

The answer is in the Fail Proof System. The answer is in stepping up as a leader whether you're officially called one or not, and whether you feel ready to do it or not. Leaders step up in times of need.

Here is how you step up.

First is brave honesty. Being bravely honest with the reality of the situation. Not trying to deny it, sugarcoat it, or ignore it. But instead to accept the truth of the reality. When we do that, we can set goals that may lift us out of it. This is a time to feel our emotions and acutely manage them with heightened attention. This is not a time to let intense emotions grab the steering wheel. Genuinely check in with yourself and with the people who need you. When we are bravely honest with tough times—whether that is industry changes, global events, or personal struggles—we're then able to set goals that can raise us out of it to a better place together. The goal then becomes our outlet. Maybe it's winning the World Cup, leading your company in a new direction, or simply sharing more connected moments with the people you love. It will bond us together as we now have something to share in as well as pour ourselves into during a time when we may otherwise feel like victims. When we have a positive outlet within our control, we are no longer helpless. We are powerful.

When it comes to these incredible triumphs, these testaments to the human spirit, the profound strength that exists within all of us—there was one shining reason that stood out above all else.

These accomplishments, every one of them, was done for others. All of these feats were achieved for other people.

After September 11, New York Yankees center fielder Bernie Williams said, "When we started playing again, I didn't see the sense in it. It seemed ridiculous to me. It only started making sense when I saw the faces of people who'd lost loved ones, people who needed this."

Needing leadership.

There is something that happens within us when other people need us. When others rely upon us, we put aside our self-focused interests and deliver our best, because they need it from us.

> **So, I ask you, right now in your life, who needs your best? A colleague, a friend, a family member. Who's looking to you for leadership?**

I know that my best self was first brought about when I was coaching those high school lacrosse players. In fact, at that time, I was wrestling with some dark areas in my life, struggling with self-confidence, and I had trouble standing up for myself. But when thirty young adults looked at me and needed my best, I found it. Not for me, but for them. The same is the case in my work now as a professional speaker. I find strength, energy, and focus in knowing that I can help better someone's life. When I'm tired or overwhelmed, I think about this impact, and I find another level.

Right now, who may need you? Give a keen eye to your work, your relationships, and your life and allow yourself to think *"Who might need me?"* I say might, because sometimes it's not always in our face with someone knocking on our door or messaging us that they need leadership. Sometimes it's you paying attention, listening, and noticing that there may be someone in your world who needs you as a leader.

This truth has only amplified as I've gone through the cancer journey with my mother. The opportunity to step up and be a positive leader for my mom during one of the most daunting and scary times of her life, and mine, has activated parts of me I didn't know were there. What's so beautiful is that it's a two-way street. People need us, and we need people. I went down to Mexico with my mom to support her there as she got the treatments she needed. When I did, I was in the middle of the hardest breakup of my life. I was heartbroken, and even though I was stepping up for my mom, my mom was also stepping up for me. That wonderful truth of us being able to lean on one another is what activated the best parts of us both.

As leaders, it's okay to need support. In fact, you will be amazed at how the people you are leading step up for you—if you let them, if you give them an opportunity, an opening. This is not weakness, this is deep strength.

As a leader—and remember you are one now, whether your job officially says it or not—it is tempting to want to be closed off, thinking of ourselves as polished and having it all figured out. But that is a misguided trap that will result in loneliness and underachieving. Show your brave honesty by being open and vulnerable with the people around you. Allow them to know you need them, and step up when they need you. That symbiotic relationship—that bond—is unstoppable.

BONDING PRODUCES RESULTS

A study by the University of Queensland in Australia focused on human bonds.[13] To do this, they had two sample groups of people and exposed one group to ideal circumstances, while the other group was exposed to difficult circumstances. The group that endured more challenging times together had higher degrees of connection, loyalty, and a willingness to put the group above themselves. The study highlighted that sharing tough experiences produces bonding. We perform because of our bond, and that bond can come from sharing difficult moments. In their one day off before competing in the playoffs, the Houston Astros went and spent time with victims of the hurricane, families that lost their homes and loved ones—forging a meaningful connection with the people they were leading. After then winning the World Series Championship, Astros shortstop Carlos Correa said, "Our fans have been through a lot [with the hurricane]. I'm just glad we could bring them some joy."[14]

You are at your best when others depend on you. The challenges, the losses, the setbacks that you will face together strengthen your connection. And when you are presented with an outlet, your performance together will show it.

> **The next time you experience a tough moment in your work, in your relationships, and in your life, see if you can use it as an opportunity to bond together, rather than break apart.**

I want to share with you a personal story that exemplified this in my life. It's a very dear and serendipitous story that came from a scary, unknown moment.

I've spoken a lot about my dad, and he is a unique individual. He is very raw with his emotions, which can stir up trouble, but when he loves you, he loves hard. Now in this story, my father becomes a pirate. I should tell you he's not usually a pirate. Just a normal guy. Well, he looks like a mash-up between Jeff Bridges as The Dude in *The Big Lebowski* mixed with the *Lord of the Rings'* Gandalf—he looks like a hippie wizard. A wizard that went to a music festival but also with the intensity and mustache of a highway trooper. (I told you, he's a unique guy.)

Now, every year, my family and I would go on a trip to the New Jersey Shore. *The Jersey Shore.* There was a show on MTV for quite a while that lent the Jersey Shore some, let's call it, *branding.* Lots of glowsticks, partying, and fist-pumping. We did not go to that part. We went to a very quaint, family-oriented town. My family and I loved this trip, and my father especially lived for it. He shined on this trip. We all could butt heads the rest of the year, but on this trip, we always shared some beautiful memories and wonderful moments together that fueled us for the times ahead. So, this trip meant a lot to each of us.

It was the first morning of the vacation. I wake up and stroll to the kitchen, but my mom isn't there. Neither is my dad. "That's odd..." I think to myself. I send my mom a message, and she responds immediately, in all capital letters, "EVERYTHING'S FINE!" A little concerning, so I write back, "What's going on?" and she says, "Dad is in the hospital. But don't worry, I also picked up bagels." I told you: my mom is a sweet Italian lady, and she just wants to feed you and love you.

I don't know what happened, but my dad came back from the hospital, and half of his face was paralyzed. He was wearing this industrial-sized eyepatch that the hospital gave him. I should tell you: he could have upgraded to a lovely, tailored eyepatch for forty dollars, but if you know dads, you know he was not going to pay forty dollars. In his words, "That is a racket down at the hospital. You give me two days. I know an eyepatch guy in Brooklyn—" I just couldn't let him finish, "Wait, you have an eyepatch guy? What are you talking about!"

For the rest of the vacation, my dad kept to himself. He was uncomfortable, upset, embarrassed, and in pain the whole trip. He locked himself away in his room; he wouldn't even be around his family the entire trip.

This trip means so much to us. Our goal was to share loving memories together. Our definition of success is to experience times together that will fill us up and fuel us for the future, and that was not happening. I knew my dad needed this, I needed it, we all needed this. Remember,

> We are not leaders only in boardrooms; we are leaders anytime people in our lives look to us and need our best.

we are at our best when other people need us and when we need them too. This is no exception. We are not leaders only in boardrooms; we are leaders anytime people in our lives look to us and need our best.

So, I went into his room, sat down on the bed next to him, and we had a bravely honest talk together about life. Not as father and son, but as two people. It was a "human under the helmet" moment. People are not just their roles. That's not just a salesperson, that's Steve! And this was the first time in my life seeing my dad as not just my dad, but a person. A person who has lived a life, made choices, and done things. Some of those things were planned, others unplanned. Like me (Accident Kid!). We had this beautiful conversation, and I could see that he started to get a little choked up crying, and I said, "Don't. Don't do it. Because if you start crying, then I'm going to start crying," and we did. We both just sat there, ugly-crying together. I finally said, "Dad, we need to share in a good experience together. We all need this." We needed a positive outlet, and it took this form. I said, "There's a sunset cocktail cruise. How great does that sound? It'll just be adults: a lovely, classy, mature evening." He reluctantly said yes.

But when we arrived at the sunset cocktail cruise, the age demographic was a little younger than we expected. We quickly find out it's not a sunset cocktail cruise for adults. It's a pirate-themed boat ride for kids. We know this because we see little kids running around with pirate hats and pirate swords and pirate eye patches. I go to the woman selling them and ask, "Can I get an eyepatch?" She says, "Is it for your…little brother?" "No, it's for my father. Just a big eyepatch guy." She tells me, "It'll be one dollar." I quickly handed her a buck, "He's going to love that!"

I gave the one-dollar pirate eyepatch to my father, and the only way to describe it is if you've ever seen a time-lapse of a flower bud bursting open and full of life. It was beautiful, and I'll never forget my Jeff Bridges, Gandalf-the-wizard father with a half-paralyzed face and a pirate eyepatch, hanging off a pirate ship surrounded by kids who think that he's a real-life pirate as he bellows out to them, "HO! HO! HO!" which is not what pirates say. That is what Santa Claus says! To this day, it's one of our most special times together.

These moments exist all around us: these little hiccups and big devastations. Regardless if your official title says leader or not, in each of these, you have the opportunity to step up, lead yourself and lead the people who look to you when they need you most—and you will be your best self because of it.

This Fail Proof System is here to accomplish your dream goals, and it is also here for you to lead from your lowest lows to your highest highs.

As you lead your life and others in it, remember that no one is immune to hard times, heartbreak, and hurt. But also remember that you're now immune to them stopping you. You are an Unstoppable Leader.

Fail Proof Keys:

» Authentically leading yourself allows you to authentically lead others.

» The lowest lows can lead to the highest highs. Be bravely honest with the situation, care for the people you are leading, and pour yourselves into a positive outlet within your control.

» The next time you experience a tough moment, see if you can use it as an opportunity to bond together, rather than break apart.

» You are at your best when others need you. You don't need to be ready, you just need to step into the opportunity—and you will become more than ready.

Fill Up Your Confidence Bank

_ _ _ _ _ _ _ _ _ _ _ _ _ _

*"Many of life's failures are people who did not realize how
close they were to success when they gave up."*
—Thomas Edison, Inventor

Confidence. What an incredible sensation. Sometimes we have
it, sometimes we don't, and sometimes we don't even know
where we'd go to find it. It's elusive, valuable, fickle, and wildly
impactful. So how do we get it, keep it, and find more of it?

As a person who's struggled with confidence my whole life,
I'd like to offer you a concept which has helped me greatly. Yes,
I struggled with confidence even while speaking on stages in
front of thousands and competing in front of the world. I have
nerves, question myself, and battle with self-belief. So, when
I tell you this concept has helped me greatly, I mean it, and I
promise it can help you too.

The Action Belief Cycle

There is an amazing relationship that occurs between two of the most powerful forces on this planet. Actions and beliefs. I call it the Action Belief Cycle.

There are two simultaneous paths as we progress toward our goals: actions and beliefs. How much we believe in ourselves, and the steps we're taking to make our dreams happen. Sometimes you will have a belief in yourself that you can accomplish the goal in front of you, but for one reason or another, your actions aren't quite there. Maybe it's busyness, or fear is being sneaky and distracting you, or you just haven't fully committed. Other times, your actions will be there. You're showing up and giving your best, but your belief is a bit low. Maybe the results aren't what you'd hope they'd be, the progress hasn't shown itself yet, and this makes you feel discouraged.

What's empowering is that the actions and beliefs are cyclical. Meaning you can lean into one, and as a result, it will lift up the other.

So, let's say your self-belief and confidence are low. If you give more energy, effort, and focus to the actions aligned with your goal, you will naturally learn, grow, and improve. As you do, your confidence will organically rise with it.

Let's say you're feeling worn down, and your actions are minimal. Focus on cultivating the belief in yourself that you are capable of doing this when the moments do arise. Make choices like the person you want to become. Think, speak, and act as the person who accomplishes this goal. Even if the grand actions are not there right now, you will be creating a foundational belief in yourself that will serve you as you do take the necessary actions. As you increase both your self-belief and your actions, you'll be making deposits into your Confidence Bank. Your Confidence Bank is the account that holds all of the factual proof of why you can and should believe in yourself. So, when fear starts voicing its opinion, you can look to your Confidence Bank and prove fear's opinion wrong with factual proof. Keep depositing these actions and beliefs into your Confidence Bank and your balance will continue to rise. You can call upon it whenever you need to for honest, grounded confidence in yourself and your abilities.

Now, I will also share that sometimes the Confidence Bank holds irregular hours. It's closed a lot. They don't have a twenty-four-seven service either, so you very well may find yourself in a time where you need your Confidence Bank, and the keycode keeps saying invalid entry. I've been there. After my rookie season competing on *American Ninja Warrior* in 2019, I decided to fully commit and give this goal everything I had leading up to the 2020 *American Ninja Warrior* season. I did the exact Fail Proof System I've given to you in this book. I was bravely honest and asked myself if I wanted this goal. The answer came back with a resounding yes. So, I committed. For nine months, I trained as hard as I could, not as a goofy host whose job it was to fail, but as an athlete whose job it is to succeed. There is no guaranteed invitation to the competition; hundreds of thousands of people apply, and only a few hundred are selected to compete. I was fortunate to be one of them. But I trained for the first six months without having that invitation, without even knowing if I'd get a shot at my goal. When I did receive it, waves of gratitude, excitement, and of course, nerves poured over me. But as we talked about here, I focused on the actions. Giving my best to the training, and in doing so, my self-belief grew with it. It filled up my

Confidence Bank. So even when my negative voice started talking smack, I could turn to the proof, and say "shush it, and look at that! In your face, fear." Adding to my firepower was the fact that my mom was going to be my guest of honor. After all of the cancer treatments, chemo beds, and tear-filled moments between us. She would now be able to stand on my sideline as I ran the course on NBC *American Ninja Warrior*. A surreal, dream goal.

On March 11, 2020, my mom flew into the Los Angeles Airport. I gave her the biggest hug of my life. On March 12, 2020, she and I went to NBC Universal Studios to do interviews together for the show. We both even did these fun, flexing hero shots to the camera, laughing all the while about what a special and memorable experience this is together. On March 13, 2020, the *American Ninja Warrior* competition was postponed due to the COVID-19 pandemic, and two days later, I broke my hand. As the hand surgeon told me, "This is a devastating injury." Wow, thanks, Doc. I was devastated. I spent months with my hand in a cast, followed by months of physical therapy, and yet again, I had to ask myself with brave honesty: Do I want to do this? Do I still want to be an American Ninja Warrior? Do I want to start back at the beginning, and commit to all the hard training *again*, work my butt off for another year without even knowing if I'll get the shot to compete?! I asked with brave honesty, and my answer came back as a deep yes.

Well, then turn to the Fail Proof System. I'm using it right now, as I've trained to come back from this devastating injury and compete on *American Ninja Warrior* 2021. The hand is healthy, and in fact, has some loving scrapes on it from intense training.

As I've had to come back from this injury, I've relied on the Action Belief Cycle. I needed to keep hold of my self-belief, even when my actions couldn't be there. When my hand was in a cast and my waistline was ever-increasing. I certainly didn't feel like an American Ninja Warrior then. When I did get back to training, after not being able to for months, my self-belief plummeted because of my poor performance. I needed to embrace the Action Belief Cycle to keep building my actions and beliefs together. More than anything, I've looked to my Confidence Bank at times in my life that I know I've given my best no matter what, and I know that if I did it then, I could do it now.

> That is why you must give your best. You *must* choose to give your best in these moments. It does not matter what the result is. It only matters that you honor the promise to yourself.

Remember, "all you can do is the best you can do." If you do this, you'll be fortifying the commitment to yourself, building up a steadfast trust in yourself, and you'll have tangible evidence to prove it to your negative and fearful voice whenever you need. When fear tries to chip away at your confidence in the future, you can turn to this evidence and say, "Look at this, fear. Here's a time I felt unsure, nervous, and had doubts, but I still did my best. If I did my best then, then I can do it now." That is powerful, inarguable, unshakeable confidence right there, and you are capable of it. As you prove this to yourself, you will have unlocked the final gate to your Fail Proof goal. If you've unlocked this truth that you can do things you didn't think you could, then where does that end? It doesn't. You are unstoppable.

Fail Proof Keys:

» Actions and beliefs are cyclical and build up one another. Lean on one, and it will lift up the other.

» Make deposits into your Confidence Bank. This is factual evidence that you can use whenever you need to prove your fear wrong.

» You've now unlocked the truth that you can do things you didn't think you could. So, where does that end? It doesn't. You are unstoppable.

Surprise Yourself

"The greatest thing you can do is surprise yourself."
—Steve Martin, Grammy-Winning Musician and Emmy-Winning Actor

You are capable of doing things you didn't think you could do, becoming someone you weren't sure you could **You are capable of surprising yourself.** be, and leading people you never thought you could reach. You are capable of surprising yourself.

In my first year competing on *American Ninja Warrior*, I even chose to have these words written across my uniform: SURPRISE YOURSELF. It's one of the greatest lessons I've learned from the sport and a lesson I'm forever grateful to have received and offer to you now. It's truly astonishing how much our brains are wired for fearful protection. Meaning, our brains would like us to stay right here, do nothing, and just be safe. Like so much of what we've talked about together, the root sentiment is fine, but it is horribly misguided.

For instance, karaoke is one of my greatest fears. Karaoke! Why, you ask? Because I'm scared I won't sing well, people will judge me, and most likely make fun of me. Okay, that's not the most ridiculous concern, but what is ridiculous is the level of paralysis and blacking out that occurs if I happen to enter a karaoke bar. Seriously, you would think there was a jungle cat on the loose in *"KC's Karaoke Club."* Do you ever have a moment like this? Maybe it's not karaoke, maybe it's giving a presentation, or dancing at a wedding, or confronting a person with a difficult conversation. A moment where our minds immediately spark up to say "No, you cannot do that! Bad things will happen!" It's a horribly outdated instinct that has very little place in our modern world. Fear is a package deal with being a person. It comes standard in the human being model. But now, your ability to realize that the fear is misguided and irrational will open up doors that once seemed sealed closed. It's liberating and empowering! By honoring our promises, and embracing the Fail Proof System, you will surprise yourself with how unstoppable you really are. You are able to do anything in this world. Anything.

This is one of the greatest thrills on Earth right there with your ability to help others surprise themselves. As an Unstoppable Leader, you will be able to instill self-belief in people, support, and challenge them to take actions to surprise themselves too. It's one of the most amazing sources of success, love, and fulfillment in this life.

You'll even start to notice this occurrence happening in the world around you, and when you do, it'll feel like you're finding more people like you in this secret Unstoppable Society. People who have chosen to keep committed, embrace failing, and relentlessly give their best—and when they did, they unlocked astounding and surprising results.

There are widely-known stories like Thomas Edison who famously proclaimed, "I have not failed. I've just found 10,000 ways that won't work." And as Nicolas Cage's character added in the film, *National Treasure*, "He just needed to find one that worked." Correct you are, Nic. You see, now as you hear that quote, you realize that in those ten thousand attempts, Edison wasn't beating his head against the wall with frustration and repetition. He was learning, growing, and improving. All the while, the above quote clearly shows his positive outlook toward achieving his goal. Why would he not quit at attempt 739? Or 9,739? I have no doubt that with brave honesty he knew how much this goal meant to him. He kept committed with big, bold actions and a rising self-belief until, finally, he achieved his target success. Thomas Edison is in our Unstoppable Society.

Have fun looking at successful people and identifying how they've used the Fail Proof System. It's invigorating, freeing, and empowering when you realize that any successful person did what we are doing right here.

Wait, Alex, then why doesn't everyone just do it? Everyone can do it. But not everyone is ready to honor the promises that it requires. That is truly the gatekeeper. But you now have the keys.

Okay, so who else did this? Who else is in our Unstoppable Society?

If you go into your garage right now, or a friend's shed, or just about any gas station, you'll see an unglamorous yet iconic product, called WD-40. What you will not see is a product called WD-39, but that is how many attempts the company had before they nailed their formula. They even respected their "failed" attempts in the name with the number forty. Every attempt, therefore, was critical to learning, growing, and improving in order to crack their formula, and in turn, become a $1.3 billion company.

In our Fail Proof System, the golden nugget piece is so critical because that is what will consistently elevate your performance—that hidden clue that you uncover gives you direction for the next step, a clue that you can only uncover by giving your best.

This Unstoppable Society is populated by success stories from every industry and walk of life. NFL Champion quarterback Kurt Warner was fired from his job and bagging groceries before he then re-committed and became a Superbowl MVP. Elvis Presley was told by his manager to quit and "go back to driving a truck." Instead, he wrote "Heartbreak Hotel" and became the King of Rock and Roll. The home rental behemoth of success, Airbnb, which revolutionized an industry and even the culture of travel, had their big launch at the South by Southwest festival and received only two bookings. Two. They're now worth $25 billion.

Now important notes here. These incredible success stories were not accomplished through sheer determination alone. It was determination with openness to learning, growing, and improving. Leaders set the culture for organizations, and with it, must be bravely honest with what is working, what isn't working, and a willingness to make those changes.

This is where having a positive outlook is critical. Positivity can sometimes be mis-viewed as that feel-good sensation that is frosting on the cake. But, remember, positivity is how you bake a better cake altogether. Positivity leads to better creativity, problem-solving, and more energy. *American Ninja Warrior* showed me the importance of having a positivity outlook—and even more so, an outlook of *play*. As kids, we have that perspective naturally. We look at a tree, and we see a leafy tower to climb. But as adults, it can feel like that vision on the world has worn away, stiffened up, or maybe even been stolen from us. Our pressures and obligations and expectations can even make it feel like there's no time for that frivolous outlook, or worse, even make us feel guilty for having fun. In your life, could you inject a little outlook of play? It can be transformative. As a kid, I never even climbed trees, now I do. Never in my life did I think I would do that (I've always been a feet-on-the-ground kind of guy). But I do now firmly have an outlook of play. Here's where it matters the most. When you are facing real conflicts or issues, having that lightness in our approach is actually an incredibly useful tactic for disempowering the intense challenge and allowing us to more effectively and creatively solve it.

| **Is there anything going on in your life right now which maybe could improve if we switch your outlook from stress and negativity to positivity and play?** |

It doesn't take the importance away from the challenge but it may just allow for better and more effective solving of the problem. There is a lot of pressure and expectations on the shoulders of leaders, and so it can be tempting to fall into the trap of stress and negativity. Indulging those emotions only leads to more stress and negativity, whereas if we stand firmly in positive energy, in making the most of any circumstance, that is when we surprise ourselves with the results; even in the most pressure-filled, stressful, and toughest of situations.

In 2009, a plane took off from La Guardia Airport in New York City at 3:24 p.m. Four minutes later, and three thousand feet into the sky, the pilot of the aircraft sent a chilling message to dispatch: "Mayday! Mayday! Mayday! We've lost both engines."

More than half a mile into the sky, the aircraft had struck a flock of birds which took out their engines. The plane began to go down. The Pilot, Chesley "Sully" Sullenberger, radioed "we're going to end up in the Hudson River."

I want you to imagine for just one moment that you are on an aircraft. *Air*-craft. Not a boat. Not even a duck-boat which can go on land and water. An aircraft. You're three thousand feet in the air, and the engines go out. You are free-falling.

We defined failure as anytime expectation does not match reality. When you purchased your window seat, having the plane go out three thousand feet in the air and tumble down to a river was probably a bit off the mark from your expectations. So, then this is a "fail."

Now I want to ask you, in this situation, would you like a negative leader? A pilot who comes on the radio, "Well, that's probably it right there for us! As you can see, we're headed toward the river, I hope you brought your swimsuits."

I highly doubt it. I bet we'd all desperately hope for a positive leader. A leader who is going to manage their emotions, problem-solve at the top of their intelligence, and be fully committed. A leader who uses our Fail Proof System.

Pilot Sully explains how he didn't indulge in distractions of fear. "I never thought about anything other than controlling the flight path and solving each problem in turn until, finally, we had solved them all." Pilot Sully landed the damaged aircraft in the middle of the Hudson River, saving all 155 people aboard.

Is Pilot Sully also incredibly gifted at this job? Absolutely. Is this example extreme? Sure. But all extremes do is more clearly exemplify truth. Extremes just pump the volume. The lesson of Pilot Sully to me is that no matter what is going on, we need to manage our emotional reactions, keep a keen eye to the golden nuggets that will help us, and be fully committed to our goal. For ourselves and the people who need us.

What might be possible if you brought this lesson to anything and everything you do? Whether it's a presentation that goes wrong, a dis-

> *If this can land a plane on a river, what could it do for you?*

agreement with a loved one, or you make a mistake in your life. If this can land a plane on a river, what could it do for you?

Fail Proof Keys:

» Your brain is wired for fearful protection, and your ability to realize that the fear is misguided will open up doors that once seemed sealed closed.

» No matter what happens, manage your emotional reactions, keep a keen eye to the golden nuggets that will help you, and be fully committed to your goal.

» By honoring our promises and embracing the Fail Proof System, you will surprise yourself with how unstoppable you really are. You are able to do anything in this world. Anything.

LOVE YOUR MOMENTS, LOVE YOUR LIFE

Your Life Is In Your Moments

‒ ‒ ‒ ‒ ‒ ‒ ‒ ‒ ‒ ‒ ‒ ‒ ‒ ‒ ‒ ‒ ‒

"I don't believe in failure. It's not failure if you enjoyed the process."
—Oprah Winfrey, Media Billionaire

Life is a series of moments, and your life is in your moments. The moments you give to your work, your relationships, and yourself, those moments become your life. So right now, it's a good idea for us to take a moment, so we can maximize your moments.

Together, we've set high-achieving goals, and you've been giving your best to making them happen. What a beautiful and powerful commitment. With that, we must also not fall victim to one of the greatest traps of our modern world: becoming future-romantics.

Now, I'm a sucker for a good rom-com movie or mushy love track. But being a future-romantic is a bit different and dangerous.

What it means is that we over-idealize the future. We can think that when we accomplish our goals, then we will feel complete, or fulfilled, or like a success. Therefore, our well-being and quality of life can be sacrificed or postponed until that future date.

Why this is a trap is because success, fulfillment, and well-being are all ever-evolving. You are ever-evolving. Even when you accomplish your goals, you will want more for yourself—as you should—but if we don't base ourselves in this present reality, then our lives will just be chasing moments that we never get a chance to live in. We will be perpetually sacrificing our current life for the future—only to then sacrifice that future life when we reach it.

This doesn't mean we pull back on our commitment, desire, or goals. There are going to be times when we need to dig in, find that extra strength, and maybe pull some late nights or early mornings. Of course, we will. Heck, I'm in one of those moments right now as I write this book to you and get set to compete again on *American Ninja Warrior*. But because I love this all so much, my fulfillment is still present—even if I'm a bit tired or beat up.

> **The key is to find that balance where you're fully committed to your future goals while also being fully present in your current reality.**

It can be a tricky balance to hit, and we're not going to be perfect at it from the start, but I've found the best access point is to honor our fifth promise. Be open to the gifts of the moment.

I know that whether it's traveling long miles to be a keynote speaker at an event or training into the wee hours of the night for *American Ninja Warrior*, it could easily feel like a "grind." But once I re-focus on the gifts of that moment, that's when I truly feel a surge in my well-being, fulfillment, and success.

Here's a quick hack into the present moment. All it takes is to shake ourselves and recalibrate. Zoom out of the current situation and look at it with fresh eyes. Try asking yourself these questions:

Where are you right now?

Who's there with you?

What are you doing and why?

Could there be any gifts in this moment? Growth, people, experiences, or opportunities?

Focus on finding these gifts. We just need to put on the right spectacles, and once we do, the gifts will appear for you. When I do this, it makes me appreciate and enjoy the moments of the journey that much more, which leads to better performing too. These moments become your life. Let's embrace your life, not endure it.

Why this is all so critical is because nothing in this life is promised. It's easy to forget that, because we live in a time of probable future. Meaning there is a high probability of us all living lives of safety, health, and longevity. But that is not a guarantee. Be bravely honest, and we both know that's the truth. In fact, I doubt you need to look far into your personal network to identify a real concrete example of how precious this life really is. If we acknowledge that truth, then postponing the quality of your life off to some distant future seems misguided and tragic.

I've mentioned my World Record, and I feel now is the time to tell you about it. Sometimes I tell people I have a World Record, and I imagine they assume it's for swimming all of the globe's great oceans while also saving them. Or being the fastest to unicycle down an ice luge. Or maybe just having an odd collection like the most left-handed spatulas. But none of those are the case, though I do have one ambidextrous spatula. My World Record was set with one of my best friends and fellow comedy-lover, Rob Mor. In 2015, Rob and I noticed that video chats from cellphones were becoming much more common. It wasn't unusual to see someone very nonchalantly video chat a person from a restaurant or while walking outside. One of our good friends, Ilya, even told us that he video chats a pal every single day. Being comedians at heart, Rob and I both naturally took it to an extreme, egging one another on, and joking about all of the different scenarios and situations that two people could video chat. Then we wondered, how *long* could two people video chat?

We did some internet searching and found out that two teenage girls in Australia had video-chatted for ten days straight and set a World Record. *Interesting.* Ten days, you say? Well, we need to beat these Aussie teens! We dug a little deeper and even reached out to *The Guinness Book of World Record. Guinness* said this would certainly create a World Record but also informed us that we'd be creating a new category, and so we'd have to pay $10,000, submit an application which they'd review six months later, at which point they may or may not approve it. Being young comedians, we replied, "If we had $10,000 and six months of patience, do you think we'd be doing this video chat?" We hung up and decided, well, *Guinness* is just a brand name, they don't own World Records. And plus, we decide what we do, right? Let's just document everything as proof, we'll already be video chatting for crying out loud! And so, we did. We committed to setting a World Record by video chatting nonstop, twenty-four hours a day for fourteen days straight—and live broadcasting it to anyone in the world! It was just like that movie *The Truman Show*.

We even looped in our buddy, Ilya, to help us. This was going to be a lot to manage. You see, our Aussie teenage foes had the video chat up in their rooms, but they were also free to leave the room and go about their lives. We weren't going to be having that. We committed to this goal of setting a world record, and so, big, bold action! We dove right in the deep end. Rob and I each had two cell phones on us at all times running the video chat, we each had wi-fi hot spots so that we'd have back up internet everywhere, and we even carried battery charging stations to make sure our digital babies were fully fed. Not to mention tripods, cables, and wires galore. Trying to leave the house with all the tech and wires felt equal parts like packing up a baby while also becoming a cyborg octopus with all the cords swinging off us. This was all necessary though because Rob was in Chicago, I was in Los Angeles, and we wanted to take this to the max. Rob took me to a Chicago Bears football game, he just propped digital-me right up there in the bleachers—what a game! I took Rob swimming in the Pacific Ocean with a waterproof case. We even performed a two-man comedy show in Hollywood. Me in human form, Rob hoisted up on a massive tripod.

The first few days were wild and so fun. Random people would want to say hi, friends came to visit, and we even did some interviews too. Not to mention the full schedules of activities to do together. After a few days though, it became a lot. This was twenty-four hours a day. Meaning even after the activities finished and people left, Rob and I would still be there together late into the night, live streaming to anyone in the world. We were never alone. I mentioned the water-proof cases, and well, we took it in the shower. Sleeping? Yup. We could sleep, but the video chat was still filming us with two cellphone cameras pointed at each of us the entire night. Nothing like waking up to strangers watching you sleep. Oh, and the restroom? Yeah, we filmed it.

> Somewhere, there is a hard drive with footage of Rob and I each in the loo. To whomever possess that footage, feel free to delete it. Please delete it.

Why do I bring this up to you now?

I remember so clearly on day nine of fourteen; I had just said goodnight to Rob. He was two hours ahead in Chicago, so I'd always say goodnight to him first, and he'd also say good morning to me. We're very close friends. When I said good-night to him, I had this realization. I remember thinking, "This is day nine. I should feel like I'm on the home stretch and almost done. But I definitely do not. This is exhausting. I feel every second, of every minute, of every hour—this is going to be brutal." But then I had another thought. I zoomed out for a moment and realized, "There will be a time when this is done. Right now, I am in the depths of it, but there will be a time soon, when I look down and this is no longer happening. So, let me be here for it now." The instant I did that, I felt this tremendous weight get lifted off of me. No longer did I feel like I needed to grit and endure through these days. I could take a breath and drop into this reality, even the tiring and tough moments, because I know it's finite. I have perspective upon it now, and so why not be here for it during the brief amount it's real. When we are present, we are open to receiving gifts.

> When we are present, we are open to receiving gifts.

I'm so thankful that I did. You see, leading up to the World Record, Rob was a best friend. We owned a production company and made films together. We were in a comedy group together, performing hundreds of shows. And we had so many heartfelt talks about our work, our relationships, and our lives. I thought we had just about every shade two best friends could have together, but when you spend twenty-four hours a day for fourteen days straight with someone, you get a wee bit closer. I'm deeply thankful that he and I did this. We accomplished something that we didn't think we could do—and didn't really even know we wanted to do it until those Aussie teens laid down the gauntlet. But in the years that followed, Rob and I have each lived our lives. Our lives are busy, they have goals, they require our heartbeats to fulfill those goals, and as a result, we don't spend as much time together. We're still life-long best friends, but the actual moments aren't there like they used to be. That's life, and that's what can and should happen as we all progress toward what's important to us. But I think back to this crazy, wild, and connective experience we had together, and I'm so deeply thankful for it, and thankful we didn't grit our teeth and endure it. We embraced it. In the hard times that he and I have each faced since then—real, hard times like losing people we love—the depth of our friendship has helped us both.

That lesson of being present in our moments even helped me get through being devastated and heartbroken to miss the 2020 season of *American Ninja Warrior* with my broken hand. I remember so clearly looking down at my hand in a cast and just thinking, "Alex, there will be a time when you look down, and this isn't here." The moments were still very difficult, but realizing the truth and having perspective upon it allowed me to be present and receive the gift of character growth. We don't need to *love* every moment, we just need to live every moment.

> *We don't need to love every moment, we just need to live every moment.*

Right now in your life, if there is something which may be causing you stress, or uncertainty, or even pain—I ask you: could you hunt for a gift? Can you be a treasure hunter right now and search these challenges for unexpected gifts? If you're looking for them, you will find them. It's like you slip on gift-vision goggles, and all of a sudden, the gifts start flashing for you to see. Now, if that's too optimistic, I can understand that, and I simply ask you to remain open to the gifts. Well, I'm asking, but it's not for me. It's for you, and it's for the people in your life.

LIFE IS WIDE

Years ago, I was reading a magazine article ranking different places to live by "Quality of Life." I started laughing. It was the first time I'd ever seen this phrase: Quality of Life. Umm... What else matters? Quality of your *life*?! It seems a bit important.

Now I don't think that a geographic location determines your quality of life. You don't need to sell your furniture and move to the tropics. I'd say that wouldn't do it at all.

| **Your quality of life is determined by knowing what you value and living your life in alignment with those values.**

If you genuinely love hitting your best quarter ever, then sipping Mai Tais off the Gulf of Mexico all day, every day is not going to be enjoyable to you. To some people, that might be heaven, but you would go crazy. Perhaps you value deep connections with your family members and friends. I have a good college buddy who lives a very simple life. I mean that in the most flattering way. He has rid his life of anything that doesn't align with his immediate values of friends and family, and as a result, he's got a wonderful quality of life because he's going off his criteria. Not yours. Not mine. *His.* So, to increase *your* quality of life, you must only be bravely honest with what *you* value and then make sure that the width of your life mirrors those values.

I say the width of life because life is both linear and wide. You have your work, your relationships, and your personal life. If we focus on achieving our well-being, fulfillment, and success across the width of life, it gives us so much more freedom—and it's much more realistic too. You don't need to satisfy all of it in just one category. Maybe your work is massively important to you, and sometimes it causes you to neglect another area of your values. Well, now that you know this, you can concentrate some effort on dialing up the volume in those needed areas, and your overall quality of life will increase as a whole. It's true that at times, we may be maxed out and something will have to lose out. But usually, that's not the case. Most times, we simply don't have the clarity of what's most important to us. So our precious few available moments get washed away into distraction, noise, or other people's values— rather than being given to what matters most to you. What I think is exciting about this truth is that it takes some pressure off of us. We can look to what we value in all areas of our lives, and by increasing any one of them, we will also improve our overall well-being, fulfillment, and success.

Let's put this into a practical example. Maybe you feel like your work and your relationships are taking up all of your time, and your self-care has really suffered. Well, now that we know that, and we know you need to take care of yourself, we can then ask the question, "What would take care of you the most?" Maybe your answer is to get a good night's sleep, or go for a long run, or just go off the grid for a day. By knowing it, now we can do it. When you have the precious availability, you will protect it, because you know you need it. And here's what's great. If you honor this aspect of you in one area of your life—self-care, in this example—then that version of you who got the sleep, or went for the run, or went off the grid is going to have an overall higher quality of life, *and* perform better in the other areas of your life. It is a deeply positive ripple.

This is vital, because we want sustained success, fulfillment, and well-being. We don't want to burn out or underperform in the future because we've been grinding ourselves too low. Showing up as a leader for yourself, your relationships, and your work is incredible, and it also takes a lot. It can be tiring, taxing, and flat-out tough. This is why we also need to make sure that we are taking care of ourselves. It will pay off now and pay off later.

If we endure these current life moments, if we grit our teeth or just go pedal down to the finish without picking up our head, then we're going to go pedal down through our lives. Going back to that analogy of climbing the mountain peak of success,

if you don't pick your head up to experience the mountain that you're climbing, it's just going to be gravel and dirt as you claw your way up. The view of life is too gorgeous for all that.

When I was hosting for NBC and I was performing stand-up, it was during the time when my highest dream was to be an entertainer and comedian. I was so immersed in what I was doing and all the distant peaks of success off in the future that I rarely picked up my head to take in the view. I remember one night at a show, a good friend and comedian came up to me and said, "Hey man, this is cool."

"What is?" I said as I checked emails that didn't need to be checked.

He put his hand on my shoulder, "You're in your dream."

I laughed at myself. He was right. I needed a good friend to tell me I was in my dream. When he did, it changed my perspective from there out. What are we looking ahead to?

POSITIVITY, PRESENCE, AND PEAK PERFORMANCE

If this was a court case, now would be my closing argument for you being positive, present, and open to the gifts. A recent study by Oxford University shows that happier individuals are 13 percent more productive than those who are discontent.[15] That means happier people get twenty-seven hours in a day. This is especially impactful when teamed with the University of Michigan's data I shared with you that states positivity leads to increased energy, problem-solving, motor skills, and overall better performance. Now, add on this research done by Dr. Laura Kubzansky out of Harvard School of Public Health.[16]

Dr. Kubzansky studied seventy thousand nurses and found that the most optimistic nurses had an estimated 15 percent longer lifespan than those who had a negative outlook. Nurses, who work long hours in intensely stressful, high stakes environments—being optimistic? If they can do that during a midnight shift in an ER, could you insert a little optimism in your life? And here's my climactic court room finale: "Members of the jury, just by being present and positive, you will receive more effective moments, better performing moments, and flat out, *more* moments of life. Plus, let's not forget, you get to actually enjoy your moments of life! Ten out of ten people agree that enjoying your life is way better than not enjoying your life." What's your verdict?

Our lives are in the moments of living. The moments of your work, your relationships, and your personal life are the moments of your life. Let's not endure your life, let's embrace your life.

Fail Proof Keys:

» Your life is in your moments. Don't fall into the trap of postponing your fulfillment, success, and well-being to a future date. Rather than enduring your moments, can you embrace your moments?

» If you're present and positive, you will be open to the gifts of the moment, you'll perform better, and you may even live longer.

» You can achieve your well-being, fulfillment, and success across the width of your life. Right now, is there an area of your life which could use some loving attention? Watch how this increases your overall quality of life with it!

You Are Unstoppable: Welcome To Your Fail Proof Life

"We are all failures—at least the best of us are."
—J.M. Barrie, Playwright & Creator of *Peter Pan*

You are now Fail Proof. You are the Unstoppable You. And I'm so honored that you have allowed me to support you on this very special, impactful, and transformative journey.

Being Fail Proof is about believing in yourself and the people with you. It's the belief that no matter what comes your way, you will persevere through it—even more than that, you will not endure it, but you will embrace it, because you know all of the wonderful, unexpected gifts it will bring to your life.

> *Being Fail Proof is about believing in yourself and the people with you.*

Keep close to our promises. They are fundamentals to living a life of well-being, fulfillment, and success. Our promises will serve you in all areas of your life—from work to your relationships to yourself. Be bravely honest. Take big, bold actions. Choose to believe in yourself. Always give your best, and be open to gifts.

Be aware of the thieves that will try to steal your joy and goals away from you. Villains like fear, **Be aware of the thieves** negativity, and uncertainty. They are sneaky, deceitful, and conspire to convince you to quit on your goals and give up on yourself. But you know how to handle them now. Trust in yourself, and use the Fail Proof System. The villains hate it because it gives you superpowers.

Set clear goals that actually matter to you and the people who need you. Then make them real, and when you do, dive in the deep end, no matter if it's a swan dive or a belly flop. Manage those emotions, and channel them as positive fuel. Keep growing, learning, and improving with your golden nuggets, and always keep committed to yourself knowing that you will become better each step of the way.

Surround yourself with floats, and remember that even when you get knocked down—or your world is knocked to the ground—you are capable of stepping up as an Unstoppable Leader for yourself and the people who need you.

In fact, you and they will both perform better as a result of leaning on one another. When you do this all, your confidence will grow, your results will grow with it, and you will surprise yourself with what you're capable of achieving. Most importantly, you will be given more gifts in this life than you ever could have imagined in so many beautiful and different ways. And when you do receive the gifts, be present with them. Your life is in your moments.

My heart swells that we've been able to share these moments together. I'm so humbled and deeply thankful to you.

I'm not good at goodbyes, so let's not make this a goodbye. I can't wait to hear about your career success written from your new fancy desk. I look forward to seeing a photo of you celebrating achievements with people you love and who love you right back. And I'm so deeply excited to meet you at an event, when you pull me aside to tell me how proud you are of what you do, who you've become, and what you lead.

From the bottom of my heart, I can't wait to witness all your Fail Proof magic in this world.

You are the Unstoppable You.

Welcome to your Fail Proof life.

CONNECT WITH ALEX!

Reach out to Alex and his team for keynote speaking, programming to facilitate your Fail Proof progress, or to share some of your exciting victories!

Connect with Alex at ImAlexWeber.com and @ImAlexWeber.

Epilogue

April 14, 2021

I wasn't planning on writing an epilogue. I turned in the book, I said "welcome to your Fail Proof life," and I went on living my Fail Proof life too. But here I am, it's April 14th, 2021, and I'm smack dab in the middle of America writing this to you as I road-trip across the country to honor our promises together. And that is why there is an epilogue.

Three nights ago, I was pouring over the final edits to this book. I'm reading and rereading our Fail Proof Promises and thinking with brave honesty over what I want for my moments of life, and what kind of leader I want to be for myself and the people who need me. A few hours earlier, I had gotten off a long phone call with my mom. She has stage four cancer and is going through her treatments as I've shared with you. Currently as I write this, there is also the COVID-19 pandemic and my mom is in a highly "at-risk" state. Our phone call was one of many that we've had to try to figure out what is the best thing we can do to protect her life. At the end of our conversation, we still hadn't come to any conclusion over what to do. I ended the phone call by saying, "Well, we need to do something." Then we hung up. Hours later, I'm in the cabin I rented in Boulder, Colorado, because I thought it would be a lovely place to finish writing this book. "I can feel like Hemingway!" But you see, I'm reading these words that I've shared with you here. Be bravely honest with yourself, commit to what matters most, and step up for people when they need you; Promises that I've asked you to honor and told you that I would honor too, especially in the tough moments. Moments where it really matters to you, but you're scared and you don't know what to do. Well, I couldn't sleep that night, and so instead of being in a cabin in Boulder, Colorado, I'm driving across the country to go be with my mom.

I'm honoring our Fail Proof Promises, and I'm also making mistakes along the way—read: *failing*. I dinged my rental car pretty good this morning. Hey, Budget Rentals, please be kind with the charge on that one, would ya?

But I also want to share with you that by honoring our promises, the fifth one is proving itself yet again. In being bravely honest, taking bold action, choosing to believe, and giving my best—I've also received so many unexpected and beautiful gifts along the way.

Old friends have called me to reconnect, I've had time to reflect and think on my next chapter of life, people I work with have even surprised me with qualities I didn't know they had in connecting and supporting me with my mom. I even got to drive by and surprise a colleague who means the world to me at her home. *American Ninja Warrior* powerhouse and my incredible friend, Maggi Thorne.

And that is why there is an epilogue. Because this is life. Your goals are evolving, challenges happen, and opportunities present themselves. Opportunities where we can indulge our negative voice of fear, back away from what matters, and quit on ourselves and the people who need us. Or, you can choose to honor our promises and embrace the Fail Proof System that will always be here as a blueprint for getting you to your goals. No matter if that's in your work, your relationships, or for your life.

Thank you for allowing me to support you to become the Unstoppable You. Now, get out there my friend, and live your Fail Proof life.

Endnotes

1 Jessica Thiefels, "5 Signs Your Fear of Failure Is Keeping You from Your Best Life," September 6, 2017, talkspace, https://www.talkspace.com/blog/5-signs-fear-failure-keeping-best-life/. Accessed May 6, 2021.

2 Magsud Rahmanov, "80% of Our Thoughts Are Negative – Control Them!" July 26, 2017, LinkedIn, https://www.linkedin.com/pulse/80-our-thoughts-negative-control-them-magsud-rahmanov. Accessed May 6, 2021.

3 Paul Rozin and Edward B. Royzman, "Negativity Bias, Negativity Dominance, and Contagion," November 1, 2001, Sage Journals, https://journals.sagepub.com/doi/10.1207/S15327957PSPR0504_2. Accessed May 6, 2021.

4 Lisa Heffernan, "Positive thinking and the power of placebo," April 17, 2019, Top Doctors.com, https://www.topdoctors.co.uk/blog/positive-thinking-and-the-power-of-placebo/. Accessed May 6, 2021.

5 Jason Murdock, "Humans Have More Than 6,000 Thoughts per Day, Psychologists Discover," July 15, 2020, *Newsweek*, https://www.newsweek.com/humans-6000-thoughts-every-day-1517963. Accessed May 6, 2021.
   Julie Tseng and Jordan Poppenk, "Brain meta-state transitions demarcate thoughts across task contexts exposing the mental noise of trait neuroticism," July 13, 2020, nature communications, https://www.nature.com/articles/s41467-020-17255-9. Accessed May 6, 2021.

6 Amy Morin, "The Toxic Effects of Negative Self-Talk," last modified February 25, 2020, verywell mind, https://www.verywellmind.com/negative-self-talk-and-how-it-affects-us-4161304. Accessed May 6, 2021.

7   University of Michigan Health System, "Pleasure And Pain: Study Shows Brain's 'Pleasure Chemical' Is Involved In Response To Pain Too," October 19, 2006, ScienceDaily, https://www.sciencedaily.com/releases/2006/10/061019094148.htm. Accessed May 6, 2021.

8   Frank Graff, "How Many Daily Decisions Do We Make?" February 7, 2018, UNC TV, http://science.unctv.org/content/reportersblog/choices. Accessed May 6, 2021.

9   Seppo E. Iso-Ahola and Charles O. Dotson, "Psychological Momentum—A Key to Continued Success," August 31, 2016, US National Library of Medicine National Institutes of Health, https://www.ncbi.nlm.nih.gov/pmc/articles/PMC5006010/. Accessed May 6, 2021.

10   Sebhia Dibra, "Mindfulness Can Increase Your Concentration and Lower Stress," October 7, 2014, PennState World Campus, https://blog.worldcampus.psu.edu/mindfulness-can-increase-your-concentration-and-lower-stress/. Accessed May 6, 2021.

11   "Understanding the stress response," last modified July 6, 2020, Harvard Health Publishing, https://www.health.harvard.edu/staying-healthy/understanding-the-stress-response. Accessed May 6, 2021.

12   Alison Wood Brooks, "Get Excited: Reappraising Pre-Performance Anxiety as Excitement," 2014, *Journal of Experimental Psychology: General*, Volume 143, Number 3, pages 1144-1158, https://www.apa.org/pubs/journals/releases/xge-a0035325.pdf. Accessed May 6, 2021.

13   Brock Bastian, "Shared Pain Brings People Together," September 9, 2014, Association for Psychological Science, https://www.psychologicalscience.org/news/releases/shared-pain-brings-people-together.html. Accessed May 6, 2021.

14   Brice Cherry, "Brice Cherry: Astros' World Series title belongs to many," November 2, 2017, *Waco Tribune-Herald*, https://wacotrib.com/sports/brice-cherry-astros-world-series-title-belongs-to-many/article_8ece2dd7-b606-5b1e-8a85-a4d3d7ce7a47.html. Accessed May 6, 2021.

15 "Happy workers are 13% more productive," October 24, 2019, University of Oxford, https://www.ox.ac.uk/news/2019-10-2 4-happy-workers-are-13-more-productive. Accessed May 6, 2021.

16 Lisa Heffernan, "Positive thinking and the power of placebo," April 17, 2019, Top Doctors.com https://www.topdoctors.co.uk/ blog/positive-thinking-and-the-power-of-placebo/. Accessed May 6, 2021.

About the Author

Alex Weber is an international keynote speaker, award-winning entertainer for NBC, and competitor on the Emmy-nominated series, *American Ninja Warrior.*

Alex has positively impacted over 3.5 million people worldwide to overcome fears, conquer challenges, and embrace failing forward to achieve their highest goals! Alex proudly wears the badge of "Failing Expert." He's a 5x TEDx Speaker, US Lacrosse Coach of the Year, and world record setter who has won awards hosting for NBC and finished as a top scorer in the World Championships of Lacrosse. With his contagious positive energy, uplifting humor, and empowering passion, Alex gives you his actionable system to be a leader in your life, realize your fullest potential, and accomplish your goals! For yourself, and for the people who need you.